The One Body of Christ

Discovering
the Truth That
Will Set You Free

KATY JEAN MARZOLF

The One Body of Christ:
Discovering the Truth That Will Set You Free

Essential Truth Publishing

Editor: Tyler Tichelaar, Superior Book Productions
Publishing Coach: Christine Gail
Cover Design and Interior Layout: Fusion Creative Works
Author Photo: Diane Schafer Photography

Library of Congress Control Number: 2022900763
Paperback ISBN: 979-8-9855843-0-1
Hardcover ISBN: 979-8-9855843-1-8
E-book ISBN: 979-8-9855843-2-5

10 9 8 7 6 5 4 3 2 1
First Edition, 2022
Printed in the United States of America

Dedication

In remembrance of my earthly mother, Jane Willmott Goodwin Ferrigno, through whom I always felt the love, support, and encouragement of God.

And to you who read this book; if it were not for you, there would be no book to write. This book has been written specifically for you, in love, and for you to know your great worth and value, at all times, and beyond time, itself.

Contents

Introduction

Though you may or may not know me, I have been sent to you for such a time as this. You may not believe reading this simple book can change your life, but it can, and it will. Each one of us is here on earth to play an important role, and as we touch one another, that profound impact is felt throughout the earth and for generations to come. Your life is important, and simply being here is all that is necessary. As you read, allow yourself to be touched and influenced for greater good. Determine right now that you will allow anything I say that helps you feel more alive to permeate your being.

You might wonder who I am that you should take my word for anything. I am no more special than anyone else. And I ask that you do not take my word. Anything I say you must be able to verify within your own experience. I will not ask you to believe anything you don't feel comfortable believing nor ask you to trust my experience. Please don't. If something is true, you must be able to see and experience it directly for yourself.

I will give you some background into how my own journey to discover truth transpired. But your story does not need to look like mine, and it most likely won't. Perhaps the only similarity might be the strong curiosity and inner desire to find truth. Maybe you are weary of being confused about how to determine what is true and what is not. Maybe you are tired of feeling hurt or disappointed by life situations.

Wherever your inspiration originates is unimportant. All you need is a sincere desire to find the truth that will finally set you free. If you keep your eyes and mind open, you will surely find it.

My background seems largely unimportant in the grand scheme of things, but perhaps it will help to explain how these conundrums can sometimes take place. For me, the question about truth came about from church and my experiences related to what I learned through the church. I was brought to church at a fairly young age, and I continued attending off-and-on with a rather casual devotion to everything church until I was introduced to Community Bible Study (CBS) when my daughters were six, three, and one. Because CBS offered a homeschool program, it seemed to work out perfectly with my homeschooling family. A one-year stint at CBS turned my casual devotion into a serious commitment. I was hooked and determined to learn and do everything according to what I believed God, through the Bible, was telling me to do. I changed my diet to be more healthy, and I stopped eating pork and shrimp. On Sundays, I attended church and read the Bible, doing as little work as possible. It goes without saying that I read my Bible every day. Anytime I felt the church was doing something that went against biblical ideals, I wrote a letter to the pastor to voice my concern. I only read books based on Scripture, and I only let my children participate in Christian-sponsored activities. We did not watch any inappropriate movies, and my children couldn't watch most of the unchristian movies their friends watched. I did all this, deeply convicted it was what God wanted from me and our family—to bring up our children with the correct values.

When I became friends with my church pastor fifteen years ago, I learned how important it was to get up at 5:30 a.m. to pray, meditate on Scripture, and memorize Scripture. For several years, I devoted myself to getting up at 4:30 a.m., praying while jogging around the neighborhood, memorizing and reciting Scripture, and praying by phone with my pastor at 5:30 a.m. daily. I was determined to put God first in everything. After two to three years of rigorous, unfailing devotion to this regimen, I'd somehow managed to memorize all of Ephesians, Philippians, Colossians 3, and numerous other complete chapters of the Bible. I even attended several Bible studies a week. I had done *everything* I knew to be close to God and to honor Him. I didn't just talk about doing these things; I lived them out. If only doing all these things had made me happy; instead, I regularly felt lonely, insecure, and depressed. My children were getting older and didn't seem to need me very much, and neither did anyone else outside the family. I kept looking for ministries to get involved in, but whatever I tried to do seemed to shut its door on me. Then…the day finally came that shook me up and turned me upside down.

I felt stunned. Even though I had seen it coming, I never really expected things to go as they did. After sending my pastor friend an email, and without any discussion with me, I received a summons to meet with the church leadership. It seemed, from my perspective, the entire committee had been overtaken by alien spirits. It was as though they had never known me before or remembered all the great times we'd shared together. To the best of my ability, I had explained I never meant any harm or ill will to the pastor by sending her the email. You may be wondering what I said. But the contents of this controversial email are truly irrelevant. What's important to know is the intention and words were misunderstood by both my pastor friend and the church leadership. And because of this misunderstanding, a great barrier was created between us. I cared greatly about my pastor friend and her well-being. How could I intentionally harm her *or* the church? The church leadership didn't see it that way, and they were concerned I might hurt her again, or continue to cause her undue stress. Perceiving a desire to see me leave, and not wanting to cause any further harm or ill feelings, I voluntarily separated myself from the church I had poured my life into for the past two years.

I was so confused. I continued to ponder and question what had been real and what had been imagined in the relationship with my friend. When we were together, I had felt so secure in our relationship. But the large lapses in her desire to spend time with me, as friends, made me question that sincerity. And after the whole ordeal with the church leadership, my heart felt ripped apart and shredded. My name and information were taken off the member-only directory. I no longer had access as a website administrator or to member-only information on the website. No one else beyond God, my husband, and my children meant more to me than my friend. I had already been intermittently depressed, but a couple of weeks after the *big bang*, I was shaken to my core.

Lying on my bed, day-after-day, I would pass the days, praying God would take me away from this pathetic life, not feeling as though anyone could possibly care one way or the other if I lived or died. In times of renewed zest for life, I prayed God would show me what was true. I asked to understand what had happened from my friend's perspective, and that we might please be reconciled. Most of all, I wanted to know truth. Whom could I trust? What could I trust? "What in this world is real?" I asked. So, weary of feeling depressed, I prayed for divine guidance to find my way out of the continual and seemingly never-ending dark fog and heaviness of mind and body.

In my quest for truth, I discovered some things of great importance. The primary one was: There is a critical distinction between relative and absolute truth.

Relative Truth: Anything that describes the changing phenomena of our experience.[1]

Declaring that something is true for one person, but not for another, is to claim that the truth is relative to or dependent on the subject being considered.[2]

If I think purple is a lovely color, that is a relative truth. Not everyone, from their viewpoint, agrees that purple is a lovely color. If I were to say airplanes are the fastest way to travel to get from one place to another on the earth, that may be true for a time, but not necessarily for all time. Certainly during the 1700s, there were no airplanes, so this statement wouldn't have been true in the past, and may not continue to be true in the future.

Absolute Truth: Absolute Truth is the ineffable and unchanging truth that transcends all concepts and language and is synonymous with Reality.[3]

In my searching, I have found the issue with relative truth to be that it is only true from certain perspectives and may not necessarily be true for all time. These kinds of truths exist in the world, but because they may change and are extremely subjective, they hold lesser value than Absolute Truth, which is true for all time, as well as beyond time. Absolute Truth is true for everyone, right now, no matter what, and, therefore, is meaningful whoever we happen to be, and at any time in our lives.

After my sweet and precious mother passed away last year, I've needed something I can hold on to, even when she is no longer with me in a physical sense. And when I lost my friend several years ago over a great misunderstanding, I needed to find something stable and real I could count on at all times. Perhaps you, too, have lost something or someone precious. Or maybe you are just frustrated by feeling insignificant, without purpose, or upset much of the time. Perchance you, like me, have been following all the traditional Christian teachings and practices, but you still feel somewhat unfulfilled, or as though there must be something more you are missing.

Read on. First, we will explore how our perspective can make a difference in how we view our world and everything in it. We will uncover the way of seeing truth in and through Christ in a way that sets us free. And with this viewpoint, we will look at several Scripture passages, including some that have previously challenged our minds.

As you read, if anything causes you to wonder about something else, or brings questions to your mind, gently lay your questions aside so you can fully concentrate on the current message at hand. If these questions persist, write them down and set them aside for later. Allow yourself to fully embrace the good news or experiential reality presented. Go beyond the words. Do not let the words I use keep you from experiencing love, peace, and joy. Instead, allow the words to wash over you and envelop you in a caring embrace. Make every effort to hear the message of reconciliation between you and everyone on this earth. You can and will be set free from the trials of this world. Trust in the process and allow yourself to feel and experience the great and mighty peace that can never be lost or taken from you, no matter what may come your way.

1

Hidden in Plain View

Seeing the police cruiser ahead, I glanced down at my speedometer, scanned the road before me, and concluded my speed seemed reasonable given the road conditions. So, when the cruiser turned on its lights and drove up behind me, I thought maybe it was just a routine check to ensure I had a current inspection and registration for my car. I turned over my information, asking if there was an issue.

"Do you know what the speed limit is?" the police officer asked.

"No, actually. I've never been on this road before." I was on my way home after picking up my middle daughter's iPod from her so my youngest daughter could use it. I'd been focused on finding a new address and returning as soon as possible so my youngest daughter wouldn't be late for her appointment out of town. With my single-minded focus, I hadn't noticed any speed limit signs.

"It's twenty-five. Didn't you see the sign?" he asked incredulously. "Look over there." He pointed.

Looking in the direction he pointed, I couldn't believe I had missed it! Two orange flags were sticking out on each side of the speed limit sign like a big warning. I was stupefied—I mean downright horrified that I could miss something so obvious! Yes, I had been focused on the mission of finding a new street, and getting there and back as soon as possible, but that sign…one would need to be almost blind to miss it! It had been there the whole time. I had just been focused on other things. And, somehow, that focus had blinded me to what should have been obvious.

This situation reminds me of another I experienced. It was a day like any other the day I got the phone call from my friend Chrissy. Not having a car, she had called for me to pick her up from Hardee's.

"Which one?" I asked. My mind was frantically trying to remember where all the Hardee's in town were located.

"The one across from McDonald's at the intersection of Carolina Beach and Shipyard," she replied.

"There is a Hardee's there?" I asked. "Is it new?" I could not, for the life of me, remember or picture a Hardee's in that location.

"No, silly," she laughed. "It's been there forever."

Not believing her, I called a friend who lived less than a mile away from that spot. She couldn't remember seeing a Hardee's at that intersection, either.

Now it's true that since moving to the area twelve years prior, I hadn't set foot in any fast-food restaurant, so I surely hadn't found a need to notice any Hardee's. I had, however, noticed the McDonald's across the street. Why had I never noticed the Hardee's before? When I went to pick up my friend, sure enough, there it was. From the outside, I could tell it had been there at least as long as I'd been living in the area. How could a place be hidden in plain view, where I traveled on an almost daily basis?

I wonder. Doesn't this sort of thing happen more often than we realize? When we go to the grocery store, how many products do we pass without learning of their existence simply because we are looking for other products? If we have a need or interest in something, it seems to capture our attention. But information or things that don't seem related to our current interests or needs are simply overlooked.

In the material and observable world, I did not see the 25-mph speed limit sign with the orange flags until it was pointed out. I didn't realize my ignorance until the police officer made the sign visible to me. And once I saw the sign in all of its brilliance, I could no longer be ignorant of it. The Hardee's was also invisible to me until I saw it with my own eyes. Thousands of other eyes had seen it and experienced the Hardee's, but I had not; therefore, I was ignorant of it. It was not that I was incapable or unworthy of seeing it. It was that I had never needed to see it, or desired to see it before. And once I saw the Hardee's, I could no longer be blind to it or ignorant of its reality. It was there the whole time, and my ignorance of it did not mean it wasn't real or didn't exist. Hardee's is now visible to me, though for a time, it was not.

It was from here—this very place of finding what I'd been overlooking—that I realized my spiritual ignorance. For spiritual ignorance is discovered in much the same way as finding previously unknown things in the material world. As we travel through our life experiences, doing the best we know how, we can miss a great many things, and never know it. Our focus and attention are in one area, so it is not without good reason that we pass over things in ignorance. Our training and life experience have brought us to this point. It has all been valuable. Without every experience, we would not be where we are today. But to go beyond where we have been and discover those things we have not been aware of, we must all take a next step into the unknown.

2

Into the Unknown

"**W**here are *you*, Gramma?" asked my three-year-old granddaughter, Aaliyah. Looking through video after video, and picture after picture on my phone, she had suddenly realized I wasn't to be seen in any of them.

"I'm the one taking the pictures, sweetie!"

Aaliyah was quiet. "But where are you?" she asked again.

"I'm there, too, sugar pea. You just can't see me because I'm the one behind the camera."

Aaliyah seemed to need to see me to prove to herself I was also present in the scene. Though she didn't appear convinced, Aaliyah didn't ask any longer about where I was. My explanation of where I was seemed simple and obvious to me, but it left me pondering. Aren't the things and events we experience in life something like the videos we watch on our TVs and computerized devices? We are here and turn on the video. We act as observers and watch some kind of story or drama unfold. Certain things happen and then end. If we are watching the videos, then we can't actually be *in* the videos, right? We can be there watching, but where are *we*? Wouldn't it be just as Aaliyah observed? We are not able to be seen, right?

We can see people. We can see emotions. We can even observe thoughts and ideas that come and go, from others, and within our own mind. But the one who sees all these things…isn't that us…the ones behind the camera?

I had thought I was a person under continual change and fluctuation, thinking and saying one thing one moment and something else in another moment. But if there is an *I* that can see and observe all this change and fluctuation, can that changing and fluctuating person be *me*? Who is the one who sees all this change? Am I not just like what Aaliyah brought to my attention…the *one* who is behind the camera…there, but not seen? Of course I am here. But anything I see and observe cannot be me, for there is still a me that is seeing and observing it all!

This discussion reminds me of a Nest Learning video our children used to watch called *The Animated Story of the Wright Brothers*. In the video, I learned how the experimenters attempting flight in the early 1900s turned out to be using an incorrect formula to calculate lift. The Smeaton coefficient had been an accepted equation for more than one hundred years, and the Lilienthal equation, which was more recently used, was also slightly in error. Only after the Wright brothers decided to set up experiments to compile their own data were they able to successfully achieve flight for the first time. All the others using the traditionally accepted formulas and models were using an incorrect premise to base their calculations and designs upon. Their viewpoints, though traditionally considered accurate, did not take into consideration what was needed to step beyond the old models that were based on the effects of staying earth-bound. In studying birds, and doing experiments in wind-tunnels, the Wright brothers took their research into the air…or heavenly realms. In the air (or heavens), and from the vantage point of being within air, new equations and viewpoints were born.

Just as in the example of the Wright brothers, if we continue to see and experience ourselves as human bodies, we will continue to have viewpoints and conclusions based on that perspective. But if we take a step into the unknown and begin to experience ourselves as the observers of all experiences, we will find our viewpoints greatly changed.

Within the Amplified Bible passage from 1 Corinthians 15:45-50, we can vividly see the necessary transition from our experiential identity as merely physical persons to that which is spiritual and unseen, like the one witnessing events behind the camera.

45 Thus it is written, the first man Adam became a living being (an individual personality); the last Adam (Christ) became a life-giving Spirit [restoring the dead to life].

46 But it is not the spiritual life which came first, but the physical and then the spiritual.

47 The first man [was] from out of earth, made of dust (earthly-minded); the second Man [is] the Lord from out of heaven.

48 Now those who are made of the dust are like him who was first made of the dust (earthly-minded); and as is [the Man] from heaven, so also [are those] who are of heaven (heavenly-minded).

49 And just as we have borne the image [of the man] of dust, so shall we and so let us also bear the image [of the Man] of heaven.

50 But I tell you this, brethren, flesh and blood cannot [become partakers of eternal salvation and] inherit or share in the kingdom of God; nor does the perishable (that which is decaying) inherit or share in the imperishable (the immortal).

From this Scripture passage, we can see that we first come to know and experience ourselves as people who change and evolve. With this experiential knowledge, everything about us is temporary and perishable.

We start out as infants. Our cells are continually dividing and changing as our physical bodies display the results of that change. In our bodies, we experience continually changing thoughts and ways of experiencing the world around us. None of it is permanent. It exists only for a period of time. Our bodies don't stay the same, and neither do the thoughts and opinions we experience.

This image, or analogy of ourselves operating in the world as the man of dust, is also perishable and subject to change. In fact, anything we can think or imagine is perishable. We do not continually think or imagine anything. While we sleep, anything we were thinking while awake is also likely to change. Thoughts and ideas come, and then they go. Though we may hang on to a belief for a time, we watch it come into our mind, and then leave our mind, as new beliefs and understandings take its place. Any ideas we can have about ourselves, God, or the world around us are all subject to change and are, therefore, perishable. And *nothing* that is perishable inherits or shares in the kingdom of God and that which is imperishable.

Did I just read that correctly in verse 50? The perishable, or that which decays or is subject to death, or some kind of ending, or annihilation, *cannot* share or partake in what is never-ending, permanent, and everlasting. So…anything about you or me that perishes, or ends in any way (our identity as persons, our flesh, blood, self-image, thoughts, ideas, emotions, memories, habits, hurts, joys, frustrations, triumphs, accomplishments, failures, etc.), cannot and will not inherit or partake of the imperishable, unchanging, and permanent, which is eternal.

⁴⁹ *And just as we have borne the image [of the man] of dust, so shall we and so let us also bear the image [of the Man] of heaven. (1 Corinthians 15:49)*

I love the wording of this verse! So *shall* we and so let us *also* bear the image of the Man of heaven! There is no mandate to *do* anything to make it so. After all, we did nothing in order to bear the image of the man of dust. It just happened naturally through the course of living.

And through the course of living so also do we bear the image of the Man of heaven. For it is only the imperishable, and what is permanent and unchanging, that inherits and partakes of what is eternal.

While the Wright brothers followed ideas and calculations based upon what happens to airplane wings while earthbound, they remained earthbound, earthy. But when airplane wings are up off the earth, in the heavens, they respond in heavenly ways. Maybe what I am understanding is that our temporary or earthly aspects cannot suddenly take on a permanent or eternal nature and perspective. Only our permanent and eternal nature can bear the image of the Man of heaven and have this *heavenly-minded* perspective. If we are looking at any aspect of life from the perspective of a temporary and changeable person, we will see things from that viewpoint. If we are looking at any aspect of life from the perspective of our unchanging and lasting self, we will see something entirely different.

The *earthy* or person perspective sees life from the conditioned human mind. Everything that has happened in the past is used to project possibilities or problems into the future. As a person, we have a perspective based on all of our experiences, which have been tempered by our individual genetic predispositions, as well as the situations we've experienced. All people are predisposed to certain genetic tendencies, and no two people are alike in this regard. If the same situation happens to two newborn babies, they will respond differently based on their inherited personalities.

A recent study determined that six-month-old babies react with increased arousal to spiders and snakes compared to fish and flowers, suggesting that stimulation representing an ancestral threat to humans induces a stress response in infants.[4] This study shows evidence of a mechanism that prepares humans to acquire specific fears of ancestral threats. So, even coming into this world, babies may have inherited certain genetic or cultural conditionings. As we experience life, our human minds and responses also become conditioned.

The *earthy* or person perspective sees individual lives that are separate from itself, that are either alike in some ways, or different in some ways. The human brain compares and judges actions based upon what it considers *right* and *wrong*. It categorizes. Because the person fluctuates constantly and is destined to die after a period of time, this point of reference lives from fear. One minute, we feel relatively secure, as money flows in, or our relationships are meeting our desires. The next minute, we can be an emotional wreck because something we value has been taken away. As a mere person, we can truly never be stable or constantly at peace. We may have an abundance of what makes us happy in life, but concurrently, we are living in fear of not having those things. These things can be taken from us in the blink of an eye. Our finances, relationships, favorable reputation in the world, good health, mental aptitude, hopes for the future, comfortable homes, etc. can all dissolve. Most of us, without realizing it, are seeking or depending upon at least one of these things to bring us comfort now or in the future.

Aaliyah wanted to see evidence of my existence, but anything that can be seen can also disappear from view. Even the things we imagine in our mind are only here for a while and then disappear because other thoughts or ideas take their place as we go about living. Though we may hold certain beliefs and understandings for quite some time, they are not constantly in our mind, or we would be unable to go about our lives. If we need to make dinner, our minds are focused on making dinner, not on what we believe about God, or whether abortion is right or not. It just isn't reasonable to continually hold several ideas in our mind when we must be focused on doing our jobs or listening to our children.

The wonderful news is even though Aaliyah could not see me in any of the pictures and videos on my phone, I still exist and was present in those scenarios. I was the one behind the camera lens viewing everything that happened.

Jesus Christ told His listeners, *"You are the light of the world. A town on a hill cannot be hidden" (Matthew 5:14).* What if He literally meant *you* are the light that makes it possible to see everything in the world? You are not one of the things *in* the world. *You* are the light that makes it possible to see the world. You are like the one behind the camera lens who sees everything in the world! A city or town on a hill cannot be hidden. It is in plain view. The speed limit sign was not hidden, and neither was the Hardee's. They were there all the time but hidden from my view simply because I had not looked for them until I had a need. It is the same way with our Spiritual self, or the *Man of heaven* spoken of in 1 Corinthians 15:45-49.

In asking yourself, "What can never be taken from me? What is here now and has been here with me my entire life, as a person, and will always be here?" you will find what is constant and True and is greater than everything that can be seen, but comes and goes.

3

Discovering What Lasts

I felt warm and happy inside. I had been driving for six hours without a break, but I felt energized and like I had only been driving for five minutes at most. At that moment, I did not want to be anywhere else, and I didn't want to be with anyone else. My friend was sleeping contently in the passenger's seat while I sang and harmonized along with the music on my CDs. Most of the time, I couldn't tell if I was hearing myself or the voices coming through the car speakers. The two seemed as one, and there was no difference. I realized I'd not eaten anything at all in hours, but I didn't feel hungry. I just felt happy and content. It wasn't often I had the opportunity to spend uninterrupted time with my friend. She led a busy life, and this special time in her presence was almost without time, it was so surreal. Though putting words to my experience seems inadequate, I thought surely I was in heaven, and I never wanted to leave this special place. But as with all experiences, it did end.

Think about a time when you felt lost in the moment, so thankful for where you were that you never once thought about what else could be, would be, or should be. You might have had a million problems or issues going on, but right then…if only for a moment…there were no problems coming to mind. You had no desire to be anywhere else or doing anything else. You were just content. Nothing needed to change in that moment. It was perfect, as it was, and you were perfect, as you were. If you were with someone else, they didn't need to change, either. They were beautiful, and so was life. In that moment, everything was as it should be, your insides overflowing love and warm feelings, everywhere you cast your vision.

Though the experience may have come and gone, has that joyful and content part of you disappeared, or is it possibly still there, just covered up by more pressing issues of the human mind? If we turn our attention inward, can we find this inner joy just by remembering our *lost-in-the-moment* experience? Let's take some time to do that now. Is it really so far from us, or is it actually with us now, even though the experience we reflect upon may have happened a long time ago? That car trip for me was six years ago, but the inner joy is still here whenever I bring it to mind. Has that joy and gratitude come and gone during the time since our experience, or has it actually been here with us the whole time, just in the background somewhere? Regardless, of whether you think it has been here all along…or not…the part of you that has witnessed the experience come and go *has* been here without fail.

In our quest to experientially discover what in this world lasts and cannot be taken from us, we cannot overlook reading Scripture for some clues. You may have read this passage many times before, but let's take another look at the New King James version of Luke 17:20-21:

20 Now when He (Jesus) was asked by the Pharisees when the Kingdom of God would come, He answered them and said, "The kingdom of God does not come with observation, 21 nor will they say, 'See here,' or 'See there!' For indeed, the Kingdom of God is within you."

The Amplified Bible says, *"the kingdom of God is within you [in your hearts] and among you [surrounding you].*

In my biblical studies, I learned that Pharisees, in general, were hypocritical religious types who liked to quote God's commands, but did not actually know how to follow-through and live out those same commands. It was their customary practice to seek out those who didn't follow all of God's rules and attempt to humiliate and dishonor them. In positioning themselves as judges over others, they gave their imagined self-images a boost. After all, whenever we issue a judgment and put others down, it puts us in the self-proclaimed superior position. Anyone who challenges our authority and expertise becomes a threat to our imagined good-standing. It is all very shaky ground to stand upon, of course, and it requires much effort to continually convince not only ourselves, but others, that we are, indeed, worthy and deserving of respect and honor. So, it came as a bit of a surprise when Jesus went to the Pharisees, of all people, and told them the kingdom of God (or heaven) was within *them.* In fact, not only was the kingdom of God among them all, but it was also within their very hearts!

Now I've had some other diligent studiers of Scripture tell me Jesus was speaking of Himself, as the kingdom of God, being in their midst. Looking at this passage again, though, with new eyes, I believe Jesus is specifically saying the Kingdom of God is not actually something that can be seen by observing it. They were standing there observing Jesus, at the time, so He could not have been speaking of His physical Self.

The Pharisees could have said, "See here," or "See there it is! There is the Kingdom of God right before us!" Instead, Jesus gave the Pharisees and us specific clues by saying the Kingdom of God cannot be seen or pointed to when it does come.

I don't know about you, but for many years now, I've imagined in my own mind what living in the kingdom of God might be like. And in my imaginings and mental conclusions, it has always been something that can be pointed to. In my mind, I say, "Ah...at last! Here it is! I'm finally living in the kingdom of God! No more sadness, no more tears, just the joy of the Lord! Hallelujah!" Even though I can't imagine exactly what living in the kingdom of God or heaven is like, I've thought it would be an experience or place I could identify as *the Kingdom of God.* I could then say, "It is here, and I am in it." Somehow, I must have missed something, though. For, in fact, Jesus tells us in this passage that we *can't* say, "Here it is," or even, "There it is!" Now if we can't observe the Kingdom of God when it comes, how can we know if and when it is here?

Could it really be as simple as what Jesus told the Pharisees? The kingdom of God is *within you*, within the very core of your existence and being. And did Jesus really mean to say it is true of the Pharisees, who were not followers or believers in Jesus, as the Son of God?

Going back to the example of *the one behind the camera* or the unseen one who is aware of everything coming and going, perhaps the reason this *one* can't be seen is because this *one* is the subject rather than the object we can see. In other words, we can only be aware of everything that appears to us. The essence and light of our beingness is always there, making it possible to see everything, but because it is from where we see, we cannot actually see it. We cannot say, "Here it is," or "There it is!" It is always here with us, allowing us to see and experience the world, but that beingness, itself, cannot be seen.

Malachi 3:6 (ESV) says: *"For I, the Lord, do not change; therefore you, O children of Jacob, are not consumed."*

It is just now occurring to me that the reason the children of Jacob are not *consumed* or able to come to some kind of *death* is because the essence of their being does not change or come to an end, either. The Lord within them cannot be consumed or come to an end, and this unchangeable fact of His immutable Presence within them is what guarantees their continuing existence. The human bodies of the children of Jacob were consumed and passed away, but the essence of their being can never die or be consumed because of God's unchanging, unending nature within their being. Everything in all of creation changes and passes away, but God does not.

Psalm 102:25-27 (ESV) reiterates the unchanging, unending nature of God.

²⁵ Of old you laid the foundation of the earth, and the heavens are the work of your hands. ²⁶ They will perish, but you will remain; they will all wear out like a garment. ²⁷ You will change them like a robe, and they will pass away, but you are the same, and your years have no end.

Anything created by God can be changed and passes away with time, but He is the only *thing* or One that continues on and cannot be consumed. If the children of Jacob cannot be consumed either, that means their essence must also be eternal, unchanging, and unending. For if the children of Jacob could end in some way, they could also be consumed. Clearly, it is on account of the Lord's inability to change that the children of Jacob are also safe from harm or any kind of change.

Change implies some kind of death or end of what was before. What does not change implies continuity unaffected by time. Everything we can point to seems to be affected by some kind of change or annihilation. However, the One who impartially witnesses and sees these changes…this One within us, has been here the whole time, and does not change or disappear.

In looking to the scientific community for answers, growing evidence supports what is common to us all, as well as lasting between us all.

In his book *The Divine Matrix*, Gregg Braden tells it like this:

> The existence of a universal field of energy that permeates our world is being thought of in very different terms—the experiments that prove its existence are so new that a single name has not yet been chosen. Regardless of what we choose to call it, however, something is definitely there. It connects everything in our world and beyond and affects us in ways that we are only beginning to understand.[5]

Braden goes on to say, "The key is that the energy connecting everything in the universe is also part of what it connects."[6]

An experiment conducted on July 4, 2012 at CERN (the European Organization for Nuclear Research) confirmed the existence of the Higgs boson, which is the fundamental particle within the Higgs field, a field that gives mass to other fundamental particles such as electrons and quarks (US Department of Energy, December 25, 2020).[7]

These exciting and recent discoveries are giving us all evidence to support what the Scriptures have been telling us about God's omnipresence and immutable Presence within all of His creation. If it weren't for the *Higgs field,* or *Divine Matrix,* as Gregg Braden has termed it, there would be no mass given to fundamental particles to create objects that we can see and observe. Based on everything I have researched, it would seem the unnamed field of Divine energy is what is most fundamental. Without it, matter would not exist.

The tricky thing about reading information about something, or hearing about discoveries made apart from your personal experience, is that without substantial proof, they can be difficult to believe and trust. So many books and internet sources are out there that it can be a challenge to determine what to believe and whether the sources are credible. And because of this, one of the most reassuring ways to find infallible truth that cannot be made obsolete with new discoveries of the religious or scientific world is to discover what is constant within your very self—what cannot be taken from you or disappear over time.

Right now, you can verify for your very self what is always here. It is so simple you can do this any time. You can close your eyes if it helps, but it is not necessary. Simply put your attention onto the heart area of your body. As you do so, you are simultaneously moving your attention away from your life problems and issues. Keep your attention here, within your heart, and breathe slowly, knowing you are in a safe place.

"You will seek me and find me, when you seek me with all your heart."
(Jeremiah 29:13 NIV)

As we feel the loving gratitude that emanates from our hearts, we can know it is what is continually there, but covered up by the veil of the human mind. We have thought it was so difficult to find God, but He has been living within us all along. *"He will never leave or forsake us" (Hebrews 13:5, Deuteronomy 31:6).* For, in fact, if He weren't in us, we would not be here in bodily form. Science has given us evidence that matter, in any form, could not exist without the field of Divine energy holding it together, as well as providing its mass.

In the past, I have interpreted Jeremiah 29:13 to mean we must fervently search for God everywhere we go and determine that at some point we will find Him. It never really occurred to me it could be as simple as putting my attention within the heart area of my body. We are told we can find God when seeking Him with our whole heart. Yes, literally use your heart, or heart-center. Leave the cares of this world behind as you center your attention in the midst of yourself.

You may be aware of your attention shifting here and there, but that is okay. Thoughts may come, and that is okay. Simply by watching your thoughts, watching your attention, and being aware of the things that come and go, you are noticing from where you can see all these things. The things and thoughts are okay. Do not focus on them. Just watch them come and then disappear. From here, in our heart-center, where the love and gratitude flow freely, we are with God and even consumed by God, until His Presence and ours cannot be differentiated. His Divine Presence is here and made real to us, whenever we shift our attention to our hearts.

As you go about your day, keep checking in with what is here with you always. Stay here as much as possible, but do not become a person trying to stay in your heart. A person could not do anything at all if it weren't for the Spirit of God making it all possible. Your task is simply to recognize what is eternal and lasting within yourself. It can never ever leave, regardless of whether you are looking at it or not. It is the essence of your being, and you cannot stop being something you always are. You can only stop being something you sometimes are. What you always are cannot be removed by mere inattention. Take heart and know this to be true. But don't take my word for it. You can verify it all yourself and know this *essence* to be True and lasting.

4

Finding the Truth That We Hold in Common

While I was sitting on the beach yesterday, a woman, who appeared to be in her sixties, approached me. She asked if I would be willing to receive prayers, and she handed me a rolled-up set of written prayers she'd made to pass out to people. Then she asked if I would be willing to hear her testimony about some Indian river rocks she had found. The story ended with her having a dream in which she was told an Indian curse had been placed upon her. Not knowing how to deal with this curse, she went to her pastor, who told her it could be removed by *praying in the name of Jesus.* And so, at the time of her speaking with me, I presumed she believed the curse had been lifted since the name *Jesus Christ* was spoken over her. I had listened intently to her message, hoping to gain whatever might be beneficial.

Later, while taking a walk, I pondered the encounter. It occurred to me that there could be countless interpretations of what had transpired in her life. Her rendition was one of many she could have shared regarding the same incidents. And then, other people, depending on their backgrounds and teachings, could interpret those same events in countless other ways.

The main reason for our encounter seemed to stem from training she had received that emphasized the importance of going out and sharing stories related to the power of Jesus Christ. She had quoted to me Revelation 12:11:

[11] And they have overcome (conquered) him by means of the blood of the Lamb and by the utterance of their testimony, for they did not love and cling to life even when faced with death [holding their lives cheap till they had to die for their witnessing]. (Amplified Classic version)

Clearly, this woman felt it was of extreme importance to make verbal statements to other people regarding her beliefs with the desired outcome of helping others hear, and potentially adopt, her point of view.

I have to wonder if that's what God has in mind? Is that truly our purpose here on earth? Aside from bringing God glory, the importance of sharing testimony is one of the prime teachings I've encountered within the Christian Church. Are we each to share our unique interpretations of the teachings we've acquired, hoping to convert others to *our* way? Is *our* way (especially if it follows some line of traditional Christian teaching), the *only* way…or the correct way? Are all others in error and born into a culture and life situation that has no value, other than to lead others to *my* way? Is that really what it means to *utter our testimony* (or *by the word of their testimony*)? Are we supposed to value our belief system so highly that we feel it's honorable to die a physical death to show our devotion to these beliefs? And is it really our mission to convert the world to our belief system?

Bear with me and take a step back to examine this whole line of reasoning, which most mainline Christians have been taught at some point. Imagine, if you will, that you were brought up Buddhist. Your whole life you've been indoctrinated into all the beliefs and teachings of your community. You've found love and you've found benefit in those teachings. Your family and your community have been Buddhists. Now, a Christian, who seems equally loving, comes your way and speaks of their beliefs and trainings, as though these are correct. Would this behavior not seem a bit presumptuous and possibly ignorantly arrogant to you, as a Buddhist?

Please understand the point I'm hoping to make. I know that if someone comes along and tries to tell you that 1 + 1 = 3, it isn't necessarily correct unless, perhaps, they are speaking of 1 pregnant person plus another is really 3. You see, even in the case of 1 + 1, there could be other ways of interpreting this seemingly simple equation. We could be speaking of 1 single person + another single person, or 1 pregnant person + a single person, or 1 pregnant person + another pregnant person, or even 1 person + a dog = 1 person. In each case, we could easily explain the correctness of these differing points of view. But to get into an argument over who is correct, never taking the time to see what is meant by each person's idea of what 1 + 1 is, would be completely fruitless. It would get us nowhere beneficial.

After all, God has given to us the message of reconciliation (2 Corinthians 5:19). God has not meant that we should divide ourselves, finding all the ways that our viewpoints differ from one another, but that we might discover what is common and uniting between us all, and focus our attention there.

Imagine, if you will, going to a Christian church service presented in a language you are unfamiliar with. Very few words, if any, will mean a thing to you. Yet those in attendance who understand this language might be whooping, hollering, and shouting exclamations you do not comprehend. They use a different name for whom they call Jesus. But you don't know this is who they are referring to. They attempt to explain in English and say _____ is Lord, and _____ is King. You *thought* this was a Christian church service, but in your eyes, they have been deceived into believing that some other entity is Lord. You argue that, "No, *Jesus* is Lord, and *Jesus* is king." They have a different name for Jesus and continue to argue that their God is king. This could go on for generations, neither party realizing they are referring to the same person, but simply using different names. Neither group of people can understand the other because of the language barrier.

This may seem borderline ridiculous, or obviously simple, until maybe you, as an American, watch *The Great British Baking Show*. Or maybe as a British person, you watch an American show and quickly realize that even though you both speak *English*, certain words and phrases being used are entirely unfamiliar. Even using the *same* language, there is great room for misunderstanding.

Could it be possible that the breakdown in communication and the major barriers between us could be, in large part, due to a misunderstanding of words? And in addition to that...could...well...could it even be possible that we *enjoy* conflict? Do you (in ignorance, of course) *want* there to be an *other*, or group of people who are *wrong*, and needing to be corrected and made into clones of yourself, believing in and seeing things from *your* point of view? I know this last point is stepping out on a limb, but hang in there and consider all the possibilities.

All of this is said to ask you to come along with me and explore what we hold in common with others, rather than the typical approach that seeks out differences and defends what is considered correct according to traditional or non-traditional viewpoints. Can we come to an agreement right here and now to make every effort to truly hear what is being said beyond the words themselves? And from there, to find what is constant and True? Together, can we discover a different kind of truth that we hold in common, rather than one that is argued so that one party is victorious and the other defeated? Is it possible we can find truth that is a win-win, rather than the typical win-lose scenario? If you are reading these words, simply waiting for an opportunity to find the error in what I say, you might want to stop reading now, for it will take you nowhere near to hearing and spreading the message of reconciliation that God has entrusted us all with. And looking to find what divides us will only add to your inner and outer turmoil. The choice is yours to make. Whatever you decide, just do it with your eyes wide open, witnessing your motives, as one might observe quarreling or loving strangers from afar. Do not become involved with the motives. Simply observe them.

What is it you truly want in the depths of your heart? Think about it deeply. Do you want to feel the itchiness of conflict and separating yourself from others, or would you rather feel the warm and tender feelings of love, compassion, and coming together? Do your thoughts and motives align with your desires of being at peace with one another, or do they bring a warring spirit to the scene? Just look and see. Focus yourself on your true desires. Pay no mind to anything that arises that isn't in alignment with your heart's deepest longings.

Imagine a world where each of us is allowed the freedom to follow after the things that interest us, without criticism from others. Feel how that feels inside of you. If you have any conflicts or issues with anyone else, imagine setting those things down. If there are tight feelings in your throat and stomach, notice that, and allow yourself to feel those feelings. Turn your attention to the center of your heart. Let your attention focus there, and allow those feelings of love in your heart to pour forth. You are choosing to feel the love in your heart right this minute, rather than focusing on mental issues. Imagine now, if there is anyone else you are aware of who holds anything against you, that they do the same thing. Is *this* what you truly want?

For so long, we have lived with the reality of being at odds with others, or those *others* who think differently than we do about COVID vaccinations, politics, religious views, homosexuality, you name it! Perhaps your way really *is* better, but how can we come to any kind of reconciliation or understanding if we are so focused on our differences that we can't see anything we hold in common, or see what could put an end to the mental division between us and those *others*? Hold on to this vision of reconciliation as we continue on, discovering what connects us all to one another.

5

Christ Is All

Today, I had lunch with some precious ladies. One of them passionately told us all about a testimony she had heard of one person's journey from being Muslim to Christian. Even though this person had grown up in a wonderfully loving family, he learned from the guidance of well-meaning Christians, who helped him interpret the Bible, that the religion of his parents was false. After telling his family that he no longer wanted to follow Muslim teachings, and that he was now a Christian, he was excommunicated from his family. The person at lunch telling the story found this to be a great victory, from the perspective that the new Christian had made the hard sacrifice of leaving his family and their false religion to *follow Christ* and the one true religion of Christianity. In fact, the way the new Christian's parents responded seemed to be even more proof of how false and barbaric their religion was that they could even consider excommunicating a beloved child! But before we are too quick to pass judgment upon the Muslim parents, I would ask if anyone has heard about or known any Christian families who have done the exact same thing to a child professing to be homosexual? Perhaps you have not, but I have heard well-meaning Christian parents speak about how not attending their professing homosexual child's wedding, and not speaking with their child, was for the purposes of hoping the resulting alienation might help that child turn away from those wrong behaviors and desires and bring the child back to them and God.

Is it possible there is yet another way? Can we become open to finding a way that seeks to nourish and enrich that which is common between us all, rather than exploiting and magnifying the differences and offenses held against one another? Scripture speaks to this possibility in the following passage:

⁹ Do not lie to one another, for you have stripped off the old (unregenerate) self with its evil practices,

¹⁰ And have clothed yourselves with the new [spiritual self], which is [ever in the process of being] renewed and remolded into [fuller and more perfect knowledge upon] knowledge after the image (the likeness) of Him Who created it.

¹¹ [In this new creation all distinctions vanish.] There is no room for and there can be neither Greek nor Jew, circumcised nor uncircumcised, [nor difference between nations whether alien] barbarians or Scythians [who are the most savage of all], nor slave or free man; but Christ is all and in all [everything and everywhere, to all men, without distinction of person]. (Colossians 3:9-11 Amplified Classic)

When I read the above passage, I understand that Christ is all there is. From what perspective can Christ be all there is? How can such a claim be made? By stripping away the old unregenerate (not renewed in heart and mind, or reborn in Spirit) person self—the self that has a beginning and an end, and is not the part of us that is continual. *That which is perishable and ends, cannot participate in what is immortal or continuous (1 Corinthians 15:50).*

It is only within the new Spiritual Self, and from this perspective, that we can see that Christ is all, and that He is within *all*, regardless of belief system or outward actions. Instead of seeing differences between religions and believing one is more true than another, I see the unifying truth that Christ is within us all. For it matters not how barbaric one person or nation is compared to another, or whether we believe it makes us better people to circumcise or not. Religious beliefs and practices make no real distinction in the new Spiritual Self. All the Spiritual Self can see is the never-ending and ever-present Truth of what always exists. Flesh and blood, behavior, and beliefs come and go within what is ever-present. The clouds come into the sky and change the appearance of the sky for a time, but the sky is always there, nevertheless. It doesn't matter to the sky if the clouds are gray or black, contain rain, or are white and puffy. The sky is still there in its entirety. The sky is intact and unaffected by the actions or appearance of the clouds. It is the same way with the Spirit of God. It is continuous and ever-present, as Christ exists within all, regardless of our actions or beliefs. However, if we see and know ourselves experientially as the temporary person, we will continue to see and view the world around us from that perspective. We will see differences and shortcomings between one and another from our temporary human mind. Again, what is temporary in nature cannot imagine or participate in what is continual and ever-present.

In past years, I spent countless hours memorizing and daily reciting the entirety of Colossians 3, but I never could understand it. I couldn't quite imagine how it was possible that barbarians and Scythians (who are the most savage of all) somehow also have Christ within them. To me, this was just further proof of my unregenerate self. From my temporary and limited human mind, I saw me (sinful and unregenerate) versus how I should be (Spiritual and like Christ). I reasoned if I was more Spiritual and closer to God, I might understand these mysteries. Never did it occur to me I already *was* this Spiritual Self, just as the Scythians were. Verse 9 gives us the admonition not to lie to one another. Speak the everlasting and always present truth of God, not the lie (temporary truth) of what is here only for a time and then disappears. We can find more evidence for this interpretational viewpoint by looking back at Colossians 3:1-5 (NIV).

¹ Since, then, you have been raised with Christ, set your hearts on things above, where Christ is, seated at the right hand of God. ² Set your minds on things above, not on earthly things. ³ For you died, and your life is now

hidden with Christ in God. ⁴ When Christ, who is your life, appears, then
you also will appear with him in glory. ⁵ Put to death, therefore, whatever
belongs to your earthly nature....

I think the clue here is that *you* died. Any separate and imagined temporal *you* that can exist apart from Christ is not ultimately real and
ever-present. Put this earthly and temporal perspective aside. Let it
end or die out. See the world from the center of your heart and beingness, where Christ is ever-present. As Christ, within the center of your
being, is raised and made prominent, *you* are also here experiencing
this reality, and *clothed* with your Christ nature. This happens quite
naturally when your attention goes from your head, and the mental
chatter that comes and goes, to the central part of your being, which
is ever-present.

Even though our physical heart is not ever-present, and will pass away
along with our physical bodies, it's interesting that scientists are just
recently discovering the intelligence within the heart. According to
PubMed.gov:

> Dr. Armour, in 1991, discovered that the heart has its "little brain"
> or "intrinsic cardiac nervous system." This "heart brain" is com-
> posed of approximately 40,000 neurons that are alike neurons in
> the brain, meaning that the heart has its own nervous system.[8]

Not only does our heart function as a little brain, but scientists have
also discovered that it functions independently from the brain, in addition to regularly communicating back and forth with the brain. In
the past, scientists have thought the brain was responsible for gov-
erning what happens within our bodies, but now, the important role
the heart plays in the health and harmony within the human body
is becoming better understood. In fact, it is only 22 days after conception that a human embryo's heart begins to beat, whereas it isn't
until 40-43 days after conception that the first electrical brain activity
occurs within the embryo. We've thought our brains and minds were

most important, but scientific research is showing our brains could not function the way they do without the heart being there first.

In the same way, our beingness in the center of our being is there before anything we see, hear, or feel appears and disappears. If it were not for our beingness, the witnessing or experiencing of anything else would not be possible.

In searching the internet, I've discovered the spelling and pronunciation of the actual word Christ varies from one language to another. Some of them look and sound like the English word Christ, but others seem completely different. It is amazing to consider that if a Chinese person were speaking about Christ in their language, I would have no idea. The Chinese word for Christ sounds so different from the English word. But aside from variations of the worldwide usage of the actual word Christ, there appear to be other religions, in addition to Christianity, that speak of this aspect of ourselves that is common to all. Different words may be used, but nevertheless, they speak to this common essence of Christ within all.

Albert Einstein has been quoted as saying, "There is no place in this new kind of physics both for the field and matter, for the field is the only reality." We could easily change the words "the field" to "Christ," and this statement would be saying the same thing as Colossians 3:11 that Christ is all and in all! "There is no place in this new kind of physics both for Christ and matter (or physical forms), for Christ is the only reality."

Buddhism is a religion that may not actually be a religion because its guidelines do not profess one true ruler but that there is divine wisdom in everyone.[9] Once again, the *divine wisdom* is what is within all.

According to the article "Commentary on Space Spirituality: An Islamic Perspective":

To the Muslim, God is everywhere; nothing exists besides His face: *To God belongs the east and the west; wherever you go there will be the presence of God. God is Omnipresent, Omniscient* (Qur'an, 2:115), and hence Muslims understand God to be available and responsive. The twofold nature of God's manifestation is understood among Muslims by seeing Him both as the absolute truth and as manifested everywhere in everything, and this understanding only exists when a Muslim reaches the next step: the *tariqa.*[10]

The *tariqa* is the Muslim spiritual path toward direct knowledge of God or Reality. So, the ability to perceive God as ever-present and never-changing, while also within what changes, is only possible once a Muslim directly experiences God. What we might call "Christ" seems to be the same as the all-pervading presence and manifestation of God for Muslims. The Arabic word for God is *Allah.* Per my research, Arabic Christians also call God, *Allah.*

According to the Himalayan Academy's article, "What Is Hinduism?":

> As a family of faiths, Hinduism upholds a wide array of perspectives on the Divine, yet all worship the one, all-pervasive Supreme Being hailed in the Upanishads. As Absolute Reality, God is unmanifest, unchanging and transcendent, the Self God, timeless, formless and spaceless. As Pure Consciousness, God is the manifest primal substance, pure love and light flowing through all form, existing everywhere in time and space as infinite intelligence and power.[11]

In Hinduism, the word for *Christ,* who is all in all, appears to be *Pure Consciousness.*

My research has made me realize if we search for ways we are similar, we will find them. While searching, I was not looking for all the ways science or religion differ in their viewpoints and practices. My eyes skimmed right over all of that. I went on a specific hunt to uncover how different people and religions express the reality of something continually present and unending, which is common to all. **For if Scripture is speaking Truth, it will not only be common to some, but to all.** An Absolute Truth may not be recognized by all, but it is something that *can be* recognized by all in the present moment, regardless of whether anyone is rich or poor, young or old, intellectually accomplished or mentally challenged, male or female, or not identified as anything or anyone in particular. Relative truth is dependent upon the position where one happens to be, but Absolute Truth just is. It is this way with Christ being all and in all. It just is, whether we experience its reality personally or not.

Let's look at yet another Bible verse that speaks of how Christ is the essence of all that exists.

He is before all things, and in Him, all things hold together. (Colossians 1:17)

I don't make this stuff up! It is here, right before our eyes! He must exist before *all* things can exist. Things cannot exist on their own. Within Him, *all* things hold together! Nothing can exist outside of Him.

Growing up within the Christian Church, I was taught we must mentally accept Christ as our personal savior so we can be saved from an eternity of separation from God. But if Scripture tells us Christ is all and in all, and that nothing can exist outside of Christ, then how could some kind of real separation or existence apart from Christ be possible? In the next chapter, we will explore some more Scripture passages related to the body of Christ that might help us to better understand these things.

6

One Body

I sat in the conference room, incredulous to what I was hearing. Apparently, the group of us there were all being laid off from the company I had devoted myself to for the past five years. I had given my heart and soul to this company and considered it my *family*. Now, faced with needing to make some cutbacks to stay financially viable, the company was discarding us as unnecessary. A million thoughts were running through my mind. It was right after Christmas, and I hadn't seen it coming. I had a greater income than my husband, and I now had a six-month-old baby girl. Where would I go? How would we make ends meet? The future seemed so uncertain, and it was all I could do to hold back the tears while I packed my belongings at my desk, while being watched.

Deep down inside, one of my greatest fears has been to feel unnecessary. I had worked so very hard at my job, hoping to prove to myself and others that I was, indeed, necessary. In this world, it rarely seems to be enough simply to exist. When meeting people and interviewing for jobs, we must have a *resume* of accomplishments and proof of our value. Nevertheless, Scripture speaks of our inclusion in the body of Christ, as well as our inestimable worth, simply because we exist. Because we exist, we have an inherently valuable part to play.

¹² Just as a body, though one, has many parts, but all its many parts form one body, so it is with Christ. ¹³ For we were all baptized by one Spirit *so as to form one body—whether Jews or Gentiles, slave or free—and we were all given the one Spirit to drink. ¹⁴ Even so the body is not made up of one part but of many.*

¹⁵ Now if the foot should say, "Because I am not a hand, I do not belong to the body," it would not for that reason stop being part of the body. ¹⁶And if the ear should say, "Because I am not an eye, I do not belong to the body," it would not for that reason stop being part of the body. ¹⁷ If the whole body were an eye, where would the sense of hearing be? If the whole body were an ear, where would the sense of smell be? ¹⁸ But in fact God has placed the parts in the body, every one of them, just as he wanted them to be. ¹⁹ If they were all one part, where would the body be? ²⁰ As it is, there are many parts, but one body.

²¹ The eye cannot say to the hand, "I don't need you!" And the head cannot say to the feet, "I don't need you!" ²² On the contrary, those parts of the body that seem to be weaker are indispensable, ²³ and the parts that we think are less honorable we treat with special honor. And the parts that are unpresentable are treated with special modesty, ²⁴ while our present-able parts need no special treatment. But God has put the body together, giving greater honor to the parts that lacked it, ²⁵ so that there should be no division in the body, but that its parts should have equal concern for each other. ²⁶ If one part suffers, every part suffers with it; if one part is honored, every part rejoices with it.

²⁷ Now you are the body of Christ, and each one of you is a part of it. (1 Corinthians 12:12-27 NIV)

I am reminded of a time, several years ago, when I injured my baby toe. It seemed such an insignificant part of my body before the injury. However, the excruciating pain emanating from that small body part informed me otherwise. I soon found out how many of the previously normal day-to-day activities were suddenly on my *no-way* list. Even driving a car became uncomfortable. My entire body was suffering on account of this injured and suffering body part. When at last that baby toe was back in operation, my whole body rejoiced and benefited from the healing and wholeness.

Although our whole body is one entity with many parts, sometimes it is difficult to imagine how different people with vastly different standards and values could possibly be a part of one body of Christ. Regarding my own family, as a body, I can understand how one family with many members, though vastly different, is joined together by blood into one family body. For two of my daughters, there came a time when they each decided they no longer wanted to be a part of our family. They wanted more freedom from the way we did things, so they intentionally separated themselves from us. Of course, in reality, they could never leave the family. They were born into this family by blood, and nothing can change that. They could decide, in their minds, they want nothing to do with us, and move away physically, but nothing they could do legally or otherwise would change their blood relation to us. It is truly just a mind-generated separation with the resulting outwardly appearing physical distancing. Since that time, our daughters have changed their minds and are now enjoying the benefits of being part of the family. It is the same exact thing with the body of Christ. Though people may not realize, want, or claim any relationship with Christ, this does *not* in any way disqualify them from being a part of the body. They just are.

[4] There is one body, and one spirit, even as ye are called in one hope of your calling; [5] One Lord, one faith, one baptism, [6] one God and Father of all, who is above all, and through all, and in you all. (Ephesians 4:4-6 King James Version)

There it is again! There is *one* God and Father of *all!* And He is above *all*, through *all*, and in you *all*. If God is in *all* and the Father of *all*, we are *all* part of His family and body, no matter what!

The earth is the Lord's and everything in it, the world, and all who live in it. (Psalm 24:1 NIV)

"Do not I fill heaven and earth?" declares the lord. (Jeremiah 23:24 NIV)

If there was more than one Spirit, more than one body, more than one baptism, more than one faith, or more than one God, we would be told right here. There is only one True and ever-present Father God, who has filled the entire universe with Himself.

Perhaps the key to understanding how this can be possible is realizing these Truths are ever-present, rather than temporary truths. **Being ever-present, God cannot die or change like all the temporary things and people of this world. Therefore, His body, which is Christ's body, is a Spiritual body made up of Himself, which is Spirit. The people contain His Spirit, and this is their True and ever-present essence, filled with Christ, and connected to God at all times, and even beyond time.**

We can so easily get caught up in all the ways we differ from one another since our differences can be interesting to the human mind, but all these differences are only on the surface.

⁷ But the LORD said to Samuel, "Do not consider his appearance or his height, for I have rejected him. The LORD does not look at the things people look at. People look at the outward appearance, but the LORD looks at the heart." (1 Samuel 16:7 NIV)

As people, we see the outward differences, but God looks at what we hold in common in the center of our beingness. The person has been *rejected*, as temporal, whereas the essence of our beingness is accepted as True and ever-present.

Close your eyes and bring your attention away from the mind into your heart. Slow your breathing somewhat and feel the calmness here. After you have shifted your focus to the center of your being, you may open your eyes or keep them closed. Picture the earth and all that is in it as your family and body. Stay here for a while and enjoy this inclusive vision. If any feelings or thoughts come up that keep you from including any person or group of people, watch those feelings and thoughts from a distance, and turn away from them. You are acknowledging those memories, feelings, and thoughts, but you are now choosing to welcome those people into your circle. Return your attention to the center of your being, whenever you notice and acknowledge any thoughts. It's okay for them to be here, also. But right now, you want to see and experience the part of you that is always here and can never be taken from you. Right now, you want to welcome everyone into your Spiritual family and body.

7

Born Again

Sitting on my bed, I feel content. Nothing is happening, and it is okay. I am living in the center of my being, and all seems right. If there are unresolved issues in my life, they are not here with me now. All that is here is a calm peace. I rest here.

Using my human mind, I think back on how things were before the *Big Bang* that turned my world upside down. I so desperately wanted to do something of worth and value to God. I didn't want to do *anything* else. "Take My Life and Let it Be…Consecrated, Lord, to Thee," was the theme of my everyday existence. In fact, I was so determined to make a difference in the world that would matter to God that I had become somewhat paralyzed, being afraid to get involved in anything of insignificance to God. I'd had amazing words of prophecy spoken over me, saying I had an even greater anointing than Kathryn Kuhlman (a great American evangelist who hosted services where many were healed). However, I hadn't healed anyone, to my knowledge, and I seemed to be a nobody in the eyes of the world. Several past friends had left me, and the one I wanted most to be my friend now didn't seem to want to spend time with me. I felt rejected and alone.

Today, I am still physically alone most of the time. I know I have friends and people who care about me, but God has graciously allowed me the opportunity to be in a place of solitude during the day, where I can write, as well as enjoy doing whatever comes my way. Instead of looking for some kind of activity or person to show me my worth and purpose, I am content to be, as I am. If I should ever accomplish something of value, or not, that is fine. I don't need that anymore. I have purpose simply by existing. I know that is enough. God will enable me to accomplish whatever needs to be accomplished. But accomplishing something of worth is no longer my specific mission on earth. **I trust that because I am here, I have purpose. What I do and accomplish will come about as I live.** I've been at home and watching my grandchildren so many Sundays that no one from church has called or texted to check on me in at least eight months. It's fine, though. With the pandemic and everyone involved in living their lives, I'm not taking it personally. I haven't been diligent in checking on others, either. If, and when, I have a close circle of friends, it will be welcome. However, I don't feel I need anything other than what I have right now. Comparing the view of my situation at this time versus before my big shake-up, it's as though I have been born again as a new person. It's a similar situation, but a completely different place of seeing.

In looking to Scripture, John 3:3-8 speaks of being born again of the Spirit.

³ Jesus replied, "Very truly I tell you, no one can see the kingdom of God unless they are born again."

⁴ "How can someone be born when they are old?" Nicodemus asked. "Surely they cannot enter a second time into their mother's womb to be born!"

⁵ Jesus answered, "Very truly I tell you, no one can enter the kingdom of God unless they are born of water and the Spirit. ⁶ Flesh gives birth to flesh, but the Spirit gives birth to spirit. ⁷ You should not be surprised at my saying, 'You must be born again.' ⁸ The wind blows wherever it pleases. You hear its sound, but you cannot tell where it comes from or where it is going. So it is with everyone born of the Spirit." (NIV)

To Nicodemus, being born meant coming into the world after being in a mother's womb. This is flesh giving birth to flesh. In this situation, we know where the body comes from and where it returns. However, Jesus spoke of a different kind of birth where Spirit gives birth to spirit. Like the wind, we can see evidence of the Spirit's existence. When we look for the source, however, we cannot point to it, or see Spirit returning from where it came. Although the flesh body has a definable beginning that can be seen and pointed to, Spirit does not. Spirit just is. It is eternal and never-ending. Flesh, because of its temporal nature and reality, cannot give birth to the Spirit or be born again of the Spirit.

Scripture goes on to explain that no one has ever gone to heaven except the One who came from heaven and has His home in heaven.

13 And yet no one has ever gone up to heaven, but there is One Who has come down from heaven—the Son of Man [Himself], Who is (dwells, has His home) in heaven. (John 3:13 Amplified Classic)

Unless it comes from heaven, it doesn't somehow end up there. Only the Spirit of God lives in heaven, comes down from heaven, and returns there.

The One who has come from heaven is not the flesh of man, but the Spirit of God, born in humankind. The Son of Man seems to refer to the Son (or Spirit Son) of God within man. In John 17, Jesus speaks not only of Himself not being of this world, but us, as well.

15 My prayer is not that you take them out of the world but that you protect them from the evil one. 16 They are not of the world, even as I am not of it. (John 17:15-16 NIV)

Jesus is saying that we are, in Truth, Spirit and not of this world, just as He is not of the world. Our flesh is temporary, but the Spirit within us is what is eternal and lasting. **The Spirit of Christ within humankind is what must be lifted up, that everyone who places their trust in their Spirit identity will have never-ending life.** It is the flesh that is dust and returns to dust. However, the Spirit of God is ever-present, constant, and True. Jesus does not pray that we be taken out of the world, but only that we be protected from the *evil one*, who comes to deceive us into thinking our identity is this voice in our head, or our person-self. This flesh person has a limited and changeable perspective that depends on its conditioning. Though we are in flesh bodies, these bodies, and the minds within the bodies, are not the essence of who we are. Jesus says we are not of this world any more than He is of this world.

In looking at people…or the flesh person, Scripture has this to say in 1 Peter 1:22-25:

²² Now that you have purified yourselves by obeying the truth so that you have sincere love for each other, love one another deeply, from the heart. ²³ For you have been born again, not of perishable seed, but of imperishable, through the living and enduring word of God. ²⁴ For,

"All people are like grass,
  and all their glory is like the flowers of the field;
the grass withers and the flowers fall,
²⁵ but the word of the Lord endures forever."
And this is the word that was preached to you. (NIV)

Obeying the truth (verse 22) is doing what comes from the center of your being, your heart-center, where Christ lives. We are told to love one another deeply from the heart. This is the only place where we can truly love others without condition and with sincerity. In this heart-center, we have been born again of the imperishable seed, the part of us that is always living and endures throughout time, as well as beyond time. This is how we are purified.

For *all* people are like grass. Their glory is like the flowers of the field. I love this! We are all beautiful, for a time, as people. But as people, we wither and fall, just like the perishable seed.

The perishable seed can be likened to the weeds in the Parable of the Weeds in Matthew 13:24-30:

²⁴ Jesus told them another parable: "The kingdom of heaven is like a man who sowed good seed in his field. ²⁵ But while everyone was sleeping, his enemy came and sowed weeds among the wheat, and went away. ²⁶ When the wheat sprouted and formed heads, then the weeds also appeared.

²⁷ "The owner's servants came to him and said, 'Sir, didn't you sow good seed in your field? Where then did the weeds come from?'

²⁸ "'An enemy did this,' he replied.

"The servants asked him, 'Do you want us to go and pull them up?'

²⁹ "'No,' he answered, 'because while you are pulling the weeds, you may uproot the wheat with them. ³⁰ Let both grow together until the harvest. At that time I will tell the harvesters: First collect the weeds and tie them in bundles to be burned; then gather the wheat and bring it into my barn.'" (NIV)

The man who sowed good seed is God, who sowed His Spirit within our hearts. While everyone was sleeping and not aware of their true identity in Christ, as their Spirit-Self, the enemy was at work deceiving us into believing we are only people. As the wheat sprouts and forms heads, we are accomplishing great and mighty things, through the Spirit of God. But this is also when the weeds appear because the person takes credit for all the things done in the flesh.

⁶³ The Spirit gives life; the flesh counts for nothing. (John 6:63)

It is not the flesh that has accomplished anything because it is the Spirit that gives life and the ability to do all things.

The servants thought it might be good to pull out the weeds, like in an ordinary garden. However, Jesus explains both must grow together until the harvest. The weeds (which are just our temporary and perishable identity) will be burned up within the True Reality of our permanent and unchanging nature as Spirit, within the Spiritual body of Christ. The harvest is when our Christ-nature is revealed to us. It has always been there. When we make the transition of experientially knowing the ever-present, never-ending part of ourselves (Spirit) more prominently than the ever-changeful, temporal person, then the weeds will be tied in bundles to be burned.

For millennia, navigators have used the North Star, Polaris, as a constant and true point of reference. The Spirit living within us refers to this same sort of constancy and stable place to view the world. Seeing the world from the shifting unstable sands of the *person*, we cannot find anything to hold on to. Our thoughts and ideas shift from moment to moment, depending on our mind-generated places of security. All of our comfort depends on attempting to remind ourselves of positive things. It can be a lot of work, trying to keep the fearful thoughts at bay. Our North Star is the part of us that is always there and takes no great effort to find. Sometimes, stormy weather may hide it, but it's always there. It is the core of our being, and not something separate from us; otherwise, we could permanently lose it. Perhaps the reason we have so much difficulty in finding this True and lasting part of ourselves is simply because we are looking somewhere else, or thinking it is something we will be able to point to and say we have *found*. **Christ has explained the kingdom of heaven is within us, within the center of our being. It is where we see from. It is not an object or place we see.**

Because the Spirit of God came to live in the human body of Jesus Christ, as a human, Jesus was fully man and also fully God. Because Jesus demonstrated and showed the evidence of His Sonship to God, the Father, we are tempted to think of, or worship Jesus, in terms of His flesh. After all, in His flesh, He gave us so many divinely inspired teachings and accomplished so many miraculous healings. But Scripture is fairly clear regarding the temporary nature of any form, or any image we may hold in our minds.

⁴ "You shall not make for yourself an image in the form of anything in heaven above or on the earth beneath or in the waters below. ⁵ You shall not bow down to them or worship them; for I, the LORD your God, am a jealous God, punishing the children for the sin of the parents to the third and fourth generation of those who hate me, ⁶ but showing love to a thousand generations of those who love me and keep my commandments. (Exodus 20:4-6 NIV)

Please remain open and hear out this line of reasoning. In looking at Exodus 20:4, keep in mind God is attempting to convey the impermanence of any form we can see or think of within heaven above or on the earth below. As wonderful as any form may be, since they all carry the glory of God *(Holy, holy, holy is the LORD Almighty; the whole earth is full of his glory." Isaiah 6:3 NIV)*, *no* form is everlasting, unchanging, and continually present. Even the glorious form of Jesus Christ is not exempt from this Truth. Paul gently attempts to explain this, as well.

¹⁶ Consequently, from now on we estimate and regard no one from a [purely] human point of view [in terms of natural standards of value]. [No] even though we once did estimate Christ from a human viewpoint and as a man, yet now [we have such knowledge of Him that] we know Him no longer [in terms of the flesh]. (2 Corinthians 5:16 Amplified Classic)

In fact, Paul takes this viewpoint one step further by suggesting that we regard *no one* from a human, flesh-person point of view. The thing is, if we continue to see and experience ourselves as a flesh-person, we will continue to see others, and Christ, this same way. Before we can make the transition to seeing and regarding everyone as Spirit, we must also come to know and experience ourselves in this way.

But let's not simply talk about it; let's do this now. Shift your attention from wherever it is to the central part of your being, where your heart resides. Take some time here. Close your eyes and slow your breathing, focusing on your breath and heart-center. You are always here as Spirit. In shifting your focus, you are not creating anything, or making anything happen. But as you rest here where it is always quiet and calm, the person and personal mind fall away. Because the person with its set of problems is not prominent here in the center of your being, you can know its temporal nature. It comes and goes off and on and is seen by you. And because you can see this *you* that comes and goes, you know it cannot be you. Anything you see is not you, but witnessed by you. This observation is not for the human mind. It cannot understand because it, itself, is observed by you, in the center of your being. Do not let the voice in your head fool you. You can hear it, so it is not you, and it does not originate with you. You are born of God, as Spirit. And in Christ, as your Spirit-Self, you can know your wholeness and what you hold in common with others.

26 For in Christ Jesus you are all sons of God through faith.

27 For as many [of you] as were baptized into Christ [into a spiritual union and communion with Christ, the Anointed One, the Messiah] have put on (clothed yourselves with) Christ.

28 There is [now no distinction] neither Jew nor Greek, there is neither slave nor free, there is not male and female; for you are all one in Christ Jesus.

29 And if you belong to Christ [are in Him Who is Abraham's Seed], then you are Abraham's offspring and [spiritual] heirs according to promise. (Galatians 3:26-29 Amplified Classic)

As you abide in Christ, distinctions and separations vanish. There is no you *and* Christ. You are *in* Christ, and a part of Christ. And here, surely you must realize you are not special or somehow better than the rest of the people of the world. They are no different than you and have this same Christ-nature living in and through them.

For in Him, we live and move and have our being. (Acts 17:28 NIV)

It is from here, and as our Spirit-Selves, we can know our purpose. What we do can take a backseat because who we are is so much more prominent. Instead of living in fear and insecurity as a fluctuating and temporal person, we can rest and abide in this peaceful and unchanging place of our Spirit-Self.

8

Living Water

As I write, the sounds of rain upon the roof and in the gutter continue in exponential proportion. All I can see out my windows is the constantly dripping overflow from the gutter saturated with pine needles and water. The rain has been almost continual for more than twenty-four hours, and its proliferation and present ongoing nature remind me that every living thing relies on water for its physical survival. I ponder the whole life cycle of water.

Water evaporates from liquid water. This vapor attaches to dust particles and eventually forms clouds. As the water droplets become too heavy to stay in the clouds, they drop to the earth in the form of rain…and so it starts all over again. It's self-sustaining and cyclic in nature.

Suddenly, I am with the Samaritan woman at the well in John 4:1-42. Jesus is explaining to the woman that all who drink the well's water will continue to thirst. Those who drink the Living water He gives never thirst because this Living water is like a continual well within them that never runs dry. Noticing Jesus' prophetic wisdom, the woman continues to ask questions about the proper place to worship. Her ancestors had always worshiped on that particular mountain…it was a tradition! But Jews had told her this wasn't good enough and the proper place to worship was in Jerusalem (which literally means city of peace). Jesus goes on to explain that the Samaritans worship what they don't have any personal experiential knowledge of. The Jews, on-the-other-hand, worship through direct experience. Nevertheless, there is coming a time, which is here now, when True worshipers will worship in Spirit and in Truth.

God is a Spirit (a spiritual Being) and those who worship Him must worship Him in spirit and in truth (reality). (John 4:24 Amplified Classic)

We can hear a lot of things from others about people we have not met. Though we may know about them, we do not know them through experience. These days, I can research almost any topic or noteworthy person on the internet. I can find out a lot of information about these topics or people. I may now know *about* them, but I do not know them through experience. I can read about jackfruit. Apparently, it has good fiber and nutrition and can substantially lower blood sugar. I have even learned it tastes like a combination of apples and bananas. A couple of years ago, I found a can of it in the store, but I never got up the ambition to try it. I had to throw it out since it passed the best by date. To this day, I know much *about* jackfruit, but I cannot say I know anything about it from direct experience. I have not actually tasted it.

The same can be said about worshiping God, the Father. For most of my adult life, I've attended quite a variety of churches and Bible studies where we would talk about and hear about God and His Son, Jesus Christ. We would sing and sometimes dance. I did not need to go to the physical city of Jerusalem…though one group of worshipers suggested, from their opinion, we need to move there because it is where all real followers of Christ must go.

In my extensive learning about God and Jesus, through church, Bible study, prayer, and all the traditional Christian methodologies, it has occurred to me that we *could* be worshiping what we do not know experientially, like what the Samaritan woman and her ancestors had been doing for generations out of tradition.

To worship God, who is Spirit, we must worship in our formless Spirit-selves, in the essence of what is True and ever-present. In this way, we meet with God in oneness, without feeling separated. If we attempt to worship God as our temporary person-selves, we are exalting an idea in our mind of who God is as a divine entity separate from and above us. As we worship an idea of who God is, we exalt temporary thought-forms. The incredibly interesting thing, though, is that as we exalt these uplifting ideas or memories, we often then find ourselves in a quiet peaceful place where there is nothing else but gratitude, love, joy, and peace. Because there is now no separate "us" imagining anything, but only this gratitude, love, joy, and peace, we are now worshiping in Spirit and in Truth. We are in the center of our being, where Christ and the Living water never run dry.

Jesus spoke of Himself as being *the way, and the truth, and the life (John 14:6)*. Knowing Himself, through direct experience, as Spirit, rather than as a temporal person-self, He knew this Spirit, as His essential Beingness, and as the way to experientially knowing the Father. He experienced Himself as Absolute Truth, which is never-changing, ever-present, in all places, at all times, and beyond time. He did not know Himself in the relative truth of a person. His person-self was just a temporary role He played. In fact, the word person comes from the Latin "persona" meaning *actor's mask*, or *character in a play*. Jesus was, and is, referring to Himself as Spirit, because this is a Truth that cannot change. In the passage below from John 14, Jesus is comforting His disciples and explaining they already do know the Father, and the way to the place where He is going because they know Him directly through experience.

[1] "Do not let your hearts be troubled. You believe in God; believe also in me. [2] My Father's house has many rooms; if that were not so, would I have told you that I am going there to prepare a place for you? [3] And if I go and prepare a place for you, I will come back and take you to be with me that you also may be where I am. [4] You know the way to the place where I am going."

⁵ Thomas said to him, "Lord, we don't know where you are going, so how can we know the way?"

⁶ Jesus answered, "I am the way and the truth and the life. No one comes to the Father except through me. ⁷ If you really know me, you will know my Father as well. From now on, you do know him and have seen him."

⁸ Philip said, "Lord, show us the Father and that will be enough for us."

⁹ Jesus answered: "Don't you know me, Philip, even after I have been among you such a long time? Anyone who has seen me has seen the Father. How can you say, 'Show us the Father'? ¹⁰ Don't you believe that I am in the Father, and that the Father is in me? The words I say to you I do not speak on my own authority. Rather, it is the Father, living in me, who is doing his work. (John 14:1-10 NIV)

Jesus made sure to emphasize it is the Father living in Him that does everything because *the flesh counts for nothing (John 6:63)*. In the same regard, *no one* can come to the Father by some work of the flesh. It is only through the work of Christ within each person that anyone can come to the Father. If Christ were not there doing the *work*, no one could come to the Father. In our temporary person-self or flesh-self, we cannot say the right words or do the right things to come to the Father. *In Him, we live and move and have our being (Acts 17:28)*. It is through the Spirit of Christ, and experientially knowing ourselves, as our ever-present Spirit selves, that we come to the Father, and Source of our being.

Jesus never meant to erect a dividing wall to exclude other religions from coming to the One True Father. Jesus claimed, *"I and the Father are One" (John 10:30 NIV)*. He did not see Himself and His Father as a duality, or two entities. Being within His Father, as Spirit, He would not have a separate body. He is part of that Spiritual body. Jesus does not see us, or those in the world, as separate from Him, either, because Spirit is *One* and cannot be divided or separated into two or more. *²² I have given them the glory that you gave me, that they may be one as we are one— ²³ I in them and you in me—so that they may be brought to complete unity (John 17:22-23 NIV).*

¹⁴ For he himself is our peace, who has made the two groups one and has destroyed the barrier, the dividing wall of hostility, ¹⁵ by setting aside in his flesh the law with its commands and regulations. His purpose was to create in himself one new humanity out of the two, thus making peace, ¹⁶ and in one body to reconcile both of them to God through the cross, by which he put to death their hostility. ¹⁷ He came and preached peace to you who were far away and peace to those who were near. ¹⁸ For through him we both have access to the Father by one Spirit. (Ephesians 2:14-18 NIV)

The purpose of Jesus Christ is to reconcile *everyone* to one another and to the Father. At the cross, the flesh dies, and the Spirit rises to prominence. In Spirit, all separations vanish. Paul is not speaking of needing to be taken out of the world in a physical sense. Jesus wanted for us to stay in the world and experience our True and lasting Spirit-nature within our physical and temporal bodies.

When Paul wrote the above letter to the Ephesians, there were only two people groups. The Jews were considered the chosen people of God, who worshiped through direct experience. The Gentiles were everyone else outside of God's family, who worshiped people, things, or ideas not able to be directly experienced. Jesus Christ, as Spirit, *is* our peace. It is His Spirit that lives within those who are aware of their own Spirit-nature and live *near* to Him. And His Spirit also lives within those who are unaware of their Spirit-nature and live *far away*. It is through Christ's Spirit and His one indivisible Spiritual body that anyone can know the Father.

When we eat and drink the things of this earth, which are temporal in nature, we will continue to hunger and thirst. The Living water that Christ gives us through the One Spirit will never end or run out. His Spirit-nature within our Spirit-nature lives on, giving us Life and well-being without end.

Take the time to set aside any mental confusion or distress, as you focus your attention once more on the center of your body. Stay there, allowing yourself to feel healed and whole. You do not need to understand anything, or *do* anything. Drink in this Living water, and know with certainty that it is always there for you. As you go about your day, remember to drink deeply from this great peace. Feel your common connection to others through this peace, and allow this bond to break down any dividing walls of hostility. Remember, often, the part of you that is constant, and trust in the unseen work of Christ to do what needs doing.

9

Another Look at the Word of God

"Does Grandpa do 'dude-in'?" my granddaughter, Alana, asked from the backseat of the car.

"What?" I replied, thinking I must have misheard her. Fortunately, we were at a stoplight, so I could turn around and watch her as she closed her eyes as if listening to music and moved her arms around.

"You know...dude-in," Alana said while jamming to her imaginary music. Since she was only six, I didn't get into a discussion about where she might have heard that word, or how it was spelled. With me not getting out into the world or watching much TV, I couldn't be sure if it is one of those new words people are using, or something she had made up. Nevertheless, I was glad she was able to use animated hand motions showing that "dude-in" must mean jamming to music, rather than her trying to use some other words I could have misunderstood.

Our conversation reminded me of a recent visit to the grocery store. I had encountered five people entering the store at the same time I was, and they were speaking excitedly in another language. I pondered how everything they said, clearly meant something powerful to them, but not understanding their language, it meant nothing to me. The words, themselves, did not seem to carry any power for me. Their excitement was conveyable, but the words, themselves, appeared to have an effect dependent upon the listener's interpretation. All the other listeners coming and going, who didn't speak their language, appeared unaffected. Because the five people could assign some kind of meaning to the words that the rest of us couldn't, it was as if they held a private invitation to a party only they could attend. Joining the party of *excitement* was possible, but the actual words being used were completely irrelevant to me.

On another occasion, my oldest daughter, Karen, and I sat watching *The Great British Baking Show* in amazement. "No, tell me it's not so!" I exclaimed. There it was. It was pudding week and some were making spotted dick. What in the world? How could there be so many divergent meanings of the same word? First of all, in America, pudding is like a sweet custard. But in the United Kingdom, pudding can be savory *or* sweet, and it is typically steamed and/or baked, the sweet puddings resembling a small cake. The traditional Yorkshire pudding is a savory accompaniment to roast beef, resembling popovers and topped with gravy. Some of the large Yorkshire puddings are filled with things like sausage or chili. Apparently, the word pudding dates back to the fourteenth-century word *poding*, which was a meat-filled animal stomach, something like a sausage. Well, how did it come to be that Americans started using the word pudding to mean something so distinctly different? And the spotted dick? Here in America, the most common meaning of the word dick is a male genital. But in the UK, spotted dick is a slightly sweet, cake-like dessert with dried fruit. It is a type of English pudding. Not here in America, my friends. And what of the English biscuit, which can be a savory cracker or a slightly sweet and crisp cookie? Biscuits in America, particularly in the Southeast, are small flakey quick breads eaten with gravy or with breakfast foods. There is truly not much similarity between the American biscuit and the English biscuit, other than flour as a main ingredient. Without other descriptive words explaining what is being spoken about, or being able to see, taste, and experience something, how could we ever communicate effectively about anything? So many words mean something entirely different from what they did even one hundred years ago.

In determining the original meaning behind the phrase *the Word of God*, there seem to be many biblical uses that may not be identical in their intended meaning. First, let us look to the very beginning, spoken of in the first chapter of the gospel of John.

¹ In the beginning [before all time] was the Word (Christ), and the Word was with God, and the Word was God Himself.

² He was present originally with God.

³ All things were made and came into existence through Him; and without Him was not even one thing made that has come into being.

⁴ In Him was Life, and the Life was the Light of men.

⁵ And the Light shines on in the darkness, for the darkness has never overpowered it [put it out or absorbed it or appropriated it, and is unreceptive to it]. (John 1:1-5 Amplified Classic)

Before even discussing what is being said in John 1:1-5, I find it interesting to note several different words or phrases are being used somewhat interchangeably to mean the same thing: *the Word, Christ, God, He, Him, Life, the Light of men, and the Light.* I've witnessed several friendly and heated debates among Christian friends over the proper name of Jesus, which some strongly feel should be *Yeshua.* I am not here to debate the issue, but merely to point out a biblical example where the actual name used is less important than the meaning behind the word. In the first five verses of the Gospel of John, eight different terms all mean essentially the same thing as *the Word.*

In the beginning, before the creation of any *thing* or form, and before time, Christ existed within God, as God. In this state, Christ must be Spirit and formless. For in order to be God, Himself, He must be unseen, unformed Spirit. If Christ had some kind of perceivable form that we could imagine, He would be part of the created and formed world. However, in the beginning, before the creation, He was with God, as Spirit. And we can't truly make an image in our minds of anything that has no form or shape. *You shall not make for yourself an image in the form of anything in heaven above or on the earth beneath or in the waters below. (Exodus 20:4 NIV)* Whether we speak of Christ or our ever-present Spirit-nature, an image in any form is inherently impossible.

All things were made through Christ. And is it possible John 1:3 is also saying no *thing* has been made without the presence of Christ within? For in Him is Life itself. Without this Life-giving Spirit, how could any *thing* or person live or have life?

This Life was the Light of men (John 1:4). So, in other words, the Life-giving Spirit within men allows them to see the world that appears before them. If it were not for this Divine Life and Light, we could not be alive *or* see and witness anything at all. The Light shines on in dark places. It can *never* be put out or overpowered by darkness, or by lack of recognition or understanding. The Light is completely unaffected by darkness of any kind. Darkness in this passage seems to refer to lack of seeing or understanding. If light allows seeing to take place, darkness keeps seeing from taking place.

Scripture then goes on to speak about John the Baptist, who was not the Light, but who came to bear witness regarding the Light. No man is the Light. Humankind is temporary and has existence for only a period of time and then passes away. The Light is Christ, in God, Who is ever-present.

⁹ There it was—the true Light [was then] coming into the world [the genuine, perfect, steadfast Light] that illumines every person.

¹⁰ He came into the world, and though the world was made through Him, the world did not recognize Him [did not know Him].

¹¹ He came to that which belonged to Him [to His own—His domain,

*creation, things, world], and they who were His own did not receive
Him and did not welcome Him.*

¹² *But to as many as did receive and welcome Him, He gave the
authority (power, privilege, right) to become the children of God, that is,
to those who believe in (adhere to, trust in, and rely on) His name—*

¹³ *Who owe their birth neither to bloods nor to the will of the flesh [that
of physical impulse] nor to the will of man [that of a natural father], but
to God. [They are born of God!] (John 1:9-13 Amplified Classic)*

Please make your way back to verse 9, where Scripture explains that
the True, genuine, steadfast Light illumines every person who enters
the world. The NIV says, "The True Light that gives Light to *everyone.*" Check other versions of Scripture and you will find that this
wondrous Christ Light gives Light to every man coming into this
world (NKJV). In order for something to be Absolute Truth with a
capital "T," it must be True for all, for all time, and beyond time.

Christ came to His own, both in the person of Jesus Christ, and as
this Life-giving Spirit Light, within all. He has not been received and
welcomed by all persons because neither His bodily Presence nor His
Spirit Presence has been recognized by all as the source and essence of
our very Being. If we can't recognize It within ourselves, it is difficult
to recognize It outside of ourselves. Seeing ourselves as flesh-persons,
we see other flesh-persons.

In verse 13, we realize those who are born of God are those who identify as Spirit beings, who have their being on account of the One God,
who has no birth or death, and does not see decay or death. Though
the person they live within has a human flesh body that was born out
of a union of two flesh bodies, those born of God directly experience themselves as Spirit, without a specific form. To be clearer, those
born of God did not come to be born of God simply by being told
they are Spirit and mentally coming to believe in this. **Those born of
God already were Spirit and have made a transition from knowing**

about themselves, through thoughts and memories in the mind, to directly experiencing their lasting and continual Spirit-nature.

While researching the Greek word *Logos*, which has been translated as *Word* in John 1:1, I found some fascinating information and quotes by Heraclitus of Ephesus, a Greek philosopher living 500 years before the birth of Jesus Christ.

Heraclitus used the term *logos* to describe the universal Law, or the principle that inherently ordered the cosmos and regulated its phenomena. According to Heraclitus:

> The Law (of the universe) is as here explained; but men are always incapable of understanding it, both before they hear it, and when they have heard it for the first time. For though all things come into being in accordance with this Law, men seem as if they had never met with it, when they meet with words (theories) and actions (processes) such as I expound, separating each thing according to its nature and explaining how it is made.
>
> Therefore one must follow (the universal Law, namely) that which is common (to all). But although the Law is universal, the majority live as if they had understanding peculiar to themselves.[12]

The New World Encyclopedia states that "Heraclitus also used the term Logos to mean the undifferentiated material substrate from which all things came: 'Listening not to me but to the Logos it is wise to agree that all [things] are one.'"[13]

How interesting that Heraclitus realized the Logos as being the underlying substance from which all things in the universe came to be. This seems to be exactly what is spoken of in John 1:1. Heraclitus also realized this Logos was a universal Law common to all, but not recognized by all men.

I cannot help but to be reminded of what Jesus said in Matthew 13:13-15:

¹³ This is why I speak to them in parables:

"Though seeing, they do not see;
though hearing, they do not hear or understand.

¹⁴ In them is fulfilled the prophecy of Isaiah:

"'You will be ever hearing but never understanding;
you will be ever seeing but never perceiving.
¹⁵ For this people's heart has become calloused;
they hardly hear with their ears,
and they have closed their eyes.
Otherwise they might see with their eyes,
hear with their ears,
understand with their hearts
and turn, and I would heal them.' (NIV)

According to what Jesus said in Matthew 13:13-15, the issue with not being able to see, hear, or understand is attributed to calloused hearts. It is not because people haven't *heard* the good news with their ears or seen miracles with their eyes.

In the past, I have thought the calloused hearts were caused by either not following the ways of God, not loving others, or being hurt by people. Now, I see the issue as living in the head and from the memory of past hurts, rather than living from the heart, or center of one's being.

Although what I speak of may seem to be just one more voiced opinion regarding how to solve the issues of humankind, the HeartMath Institute has devoted its resources to discovering a scientific understanding of how the heart operates and plays a part in the overall well-being of humanity. I found this information on the HeartMath Institute's website.

The mission of the HeartMath Institute is to help people bring their physical, mental and emotional systems into balanced alignment with their heart's intuitive guidance. This unfolds the path for becoming heart-empowered individuals who choose the way of love, which they demonstrate through compassionate care for the well-being of themselves, others and Planet Earth.

HeartMath Institute is committed to helping awaken the heart of humanity. We believe that when we align and connect our hearts and minds and connect with others, we awaken the higher mental, emotional and spiritual capacities that frequently lie dormant. HMI aspires to always conduct our operations with passion, compassion and a heartfelt desire to transform lives. This is in keeping with our desire to help usher in an era of ever-expanding heart intelligence.[14]

This excerpt is meant to show there are organizations in our world that have discovered the possibilities of transforming the world simply through heart-brain coherence. In the days Jesus walked the earth, we didn't have the technology to show what Jesus spoke about in a scientific way. But now there are organizations that use slightly different words to help bring us all together by awakening the heart of humanity. When we no longer have calloused hearts, we are able to see, hear, understand, and be healed.

In an article in *Science of the Heart: Exploring the Role of the Heart in Human Performance, Volume 2,* Rollin McCraty, PhD, writes about new findings and data related to the heart:

To this point, we have reviewed research findings showing that the heart's electromagnetic field plays a direct role in psychophysiological communication within and between individuals. But there are also new data suggesting that the heart's field is directly involved in intuitive perception, through its coupling to an energetic information field outside the bounds of space and time. Using a rigorous experimental design, we found compelling evidence that both the heart and brain receive and respond to information about a future event before the event actually happens. Even more surprising was our finding that the heart appears to receive this "intuitive" information before the brain. This suggests that the heart's field is linked to a more subtle energetic field that contains information on objects and events remote in space or ahead in time. Called by Karl Pribram and others the "spectral domain," this is a fundamental order of potential energy that enfolds space and time, and is thought to be the basis for our consciousness of "the whole."[15]

Considering that this research is scientifically measurable and speaks of the heart's direct connection with an energetic field outside of space and time, giving us intuitive information, we could not otherwise know, I am speechless! To me, this means that scientific equipment is now able to show and prove how we, as temporal fleshly beings, are directly connected through our physical hearts to God, who is eternal, ever-present, and within all time, as well as outside and beyond all time!

[6] For God, who said, "Let light shine out of darkness," made his light shine in our hearts to give us the light of the knowledge of God's glory displayed in the face of Christ. (2 Corinthians 4:6 NIV)

Returning to *the Word of God* or Logos, which is the genuine, perfect, and steadfast Light that illumines every person, this very Light is what makes it possible even to see the person-self. This Logos Christ Light is the part of us that is steadfast and genuine.

I have been taught that the *Word of God* is the *Bible* or *Holy words spoken from God* to a person. However, I now realize words, even if Holy, still need interpretation. The words are but symbols representing what is real. When I say the word *heart*, the word, itself, is not the heart. As I write about the heart, you will need to form an image in your mind of a heart. If you are a small child who has not yet learned what a heart is, the word will mean absolutely nothing to you. Only after being introduced to the word in association with an object can an image or understanding of the mind take place. In the beginning, before any word or word association can take place, the Word of God, or Christ, is living and present.

12 For the word of God is alive and active. Sharper than any double-edged sword, it penetrates even to dividing soul and spirit, joints and marrow; it judges the thoughts and attitudes of the heart. 13 Nothing in all creation is hidden from God's sight. Everything is uncovered and laid bare before the eyes of him to whom we must give account. (Hebrews 4:12-13 NIV)

Note that every *thing* is seen by the eyes of God. And every thought and attitude of the heart can be seen for what it truly is, which is temporary, and seen within the constancy of what is ever-present and everlasting. What is constant and everlasting is within us *now*. We do not need to form a mental image or associate any words to anything in particular to know this *Word of God*, within us, through direct experience.

Once again, bring your attention to the center of your being. Dwell here. Breathe from here. Watch thoughts appear from here. Respond to people from here. From here, you are not only a person, but the Spirit being within the person-self. The One who sees it all, and is always here within you, is your constantly True Self. The one you can see having problems cannot be your True Self or nature, because it comes and goes, and can be seen by you. Sure, that self is here for a while, but it does not stay and is not constant or consistent. That idea you have of who you are is the cause of your insecurity. Remain in the center of your being. Stay here and experience everything else as temporary and fleeting.

The *Word of God* came to many in Scripture. And used in this way, it seems to have come as spoken words. But first, the *Word of God* was revealed, and then the words came to express the message. When the formless *Word of God* is *proclaimed*, it is made known, or revealed. The Spirit Presence, which is ever-present within us, must be revealed or made known before words or ideas can come forth to express this great wisdom, peace, and love. We are so used to communicating with words that, sometimes, we forget communication and direct experience happens before, during, and after the time when words appear. Let us now take another look at the Name of Jesus.

10

The Name of Jesus

In the Bible, many of the people who experienced a time of struggle and then revelation from God underwent a name change. About thirteen years ago, I felt as though God was speaking to me through these examples and that I, too, would experience a shift and the resulting name change. I immediately thought of my oldest daughter, Karen, who has a gift for coming up with unique and appropriate names for our bicycles, cars, garden plants, and numerous other things I didn't even realize need a name. I explained to God that I didn't have that gift, so I would be needing some help to identify my new name.

Not long after, my friend Pam brought me to an evening church service with a prophetic female preacher. I had no way of knowing previously that it was the preacher's custom to call all new visitors up and give them a prophetic word of encouragement in their gifts.

"Kathryn, come on up here," I heard the pastor say.

No one went up. She was looking in my direction, but I assumed she was speaking to someone behind me since I'd already been introduced prior to the service as Jean.

"Kathryn, you, in the pink sweater, I'm speaking to you to have you come up here," the pastor called out again.

I looked down, surprised to find I was wearing a pink sweater, and realized she was looking directly at me. I walked up front, not sure what was about to happen. She closed her eyes and started speaking in her prayer language. Then amazing words followed.

"You have the anointing of Kathryn Kuhlman. Many people will be healed by you. In fact, you will not even need to lay hands on people and they will be healed. You will write great and mighty books…such penmanship has never been seen before!"

I was astounded. Only in my prayer time had I asked to be used by God to heal others. How could she have known it was my heart's desire? I didn't know much about Kathryn Kuhlman at the time, but I later discovered she had been a well-known preacher and evangelist who spoke with great faith about the healing powers of God, and many who came to her meetings were miraculously healed of all kinds of ailments.

After this event, I was high on life. I had no idea someone as insignificant as me could somehow turn out to be significant. I called my pastor friend immediately. She knew all about the ministry of Kathryn Kuhlman. Before long, she began calling me Kathryn Jean, and then finally Katy Jean. I hadn't told her about the name change from God. That had been a private thing I'd kept to myself. She would call me Katy Jean from then on, except for when I felt insecure and upset about something. Then it seemed insulting to be downgraded to just plain Jean, and I wondered if I was just making all my specialness up to feel better about myself.

One day, in early spring, when I went outside, I noticed one of the three hanging potted petunia plants was empty. Nothing at all was growing in it from the summer before. Remembering the prophetic words about my gift of healing, I reached up and prayed over that plant to be even more beautiful than before. Expecting instantaneous results, I was disappointed to find nothing growing after three days. I stopped looking, afraid to be reminded of my failure and lack of healing ability. Then on Mother's Day, seven weeks later, my husband looked over to the plant as we were about to start our walk.

"What's that?" he exclaimed.

We both went over to look, amazed to find not only a beautifully green petunia plant thriving in the pot I'd prayed over, but also one plant in the middle with one pure white bloom and several white buds, surrounded by plants with fuchsia blooms. "How could this be?" I wondered. The original plants had all been fuchsia-colored blooms. I've since been told that colored plants often come from white ones. However, to go from colored to pure white is extremely uncommon. I remembered the meaning of the name Kathryn or Katy as being *pure*. Once again, I saw the hand of God at work in showing me my true pure nature, and I was filled with enthusiasm and zest for the purpose of my life.

But as challenges and emotional trouble came my way, I returned to questioning the purpose for my being on earth. I sank to an all-time low as I arrived at another conference with my friend, Pam, only to find out my pre-made nametag said only *Jean*. My friend told me she didn't know what had happened. She had registered me as *Katy Jean*. I handwrote *Katy* with a regular pen in front of the Sharpie pre-written *Jean*. At the prophetic reading, I expected nothing. I sat there patiently waiting for my turn. The person speaking words about me couldn't read my nametag because of her distance from me.

"You, there. I can't read your name. God has given you a new name. Walk in it and know it to be true."

When I began going by my new nickname of Katy Jean, my parents thought I didn't like the name they had given me. They didn't understand this was not the case. I wanted them to realize I had gone through a shift and was now different than before. I wasn't the one who had wanted a new name. The new name was given to me by others as a reminder, from God, of my true nature.

At the time, those experiences gave me an ego boost. To feel good about myself, I needed to feel better than others. Even though I probably didn't realize this was the case, it was. I can see it now. I didn't want to be just ordinary. Feeling my life had a noticeable purpose that could be identified and pointed to seemed necessary at the time. It was the only thing that kept me getting up and going every day. In essence, I needed to *make a name for myself* that involved performing a tangible contribution to the world that would validate the necessity of my existence. If I contributed nothing of significance and nothing to remember, I reasoned, there would be no point for my life. I was continually looking for others, and the world, to validate my purpose and ongoing existence. When I didn't see evidence of that confirmation, I believed I had no purpose for being on the earth.

Today, at this point in my journey, the actual name people call me is somewhat unimportant. I've been mistakenly called my daughters' and sister's names, and even my pastor friend's name. The actual name is not my identity, though.

Dictionary.com says a name is: "a word or a combination of words by which a person, place, or thing, a body or class, or any object of thought is designated, called, or known."[16]

In reality, the name *of* something is not the actual thing. I, as the subject, see, hear, or sense a thing that is not me, and therefore, I have a need to identify or refer to that person, place, or thing by using some kind of language or symbol. Often, when I am talking with someone, one of us has trouble remembering the actual name of a person or object, so we need to use other descriptive words to help the other understand whom or what we are referring to. The actual name or descriptive words we use are less important than the end result of communicating a specific idea to another person. No matter what name anyone calls me, I am still the same. The actual name cannot change who I am.

In *Romeo and Juliet*, Shakespeare had Juliet speak to Romeo with these words: *"What's in a name? That which we call a rose by any other name would smell as sweet."* Juliet had realized her deep love for Romeo, which was of greater importance than his family name. It was only the remembrance of what his family name and her family name signified that stood in the way of their happiness together. If they could forget all the history centered around the feud between their families, all that would remain would be their love for each other. Regardless of the actual name used for a rose, or for Romeo, its true nature and fragrance would still be sweet.

I have realized my true nature cannot be changed simply by the words or names someone uses to refer to me. Others may think well of me… or not, but my essence remains unchanged. Only the human mind is affected by the name, during the process of attempting to give positive or negative meaning to the words.

In the case of Jesus Christ, at first glance, it may seem obvious what His name is. But if we investigate further, we will find some other possibilities mentioned in Scripture. Most importantly, let's look at what Jesus said about His name.

I will remain in the world no longer, but they are still in the world, and I am coming to you. Holy Father, protect them by the power of your name, the name you gave me, so that they may be one as we are one. (John 17:11 NIV)

In this passage, Jesus says His name is the name His Father gave Him, which is *also* the name of His Father. And not only is Jesus' name the same as His Father's name, but it is the name behind the power that protects us in the world, and also the name that causes us to be one, in the same way that Jesus and His Father are one.

If there is any doubt about Jesus' name being one and the same as His Father's name, search the Scriptures for evidence. Here it is again.

Jesus answered, "I did tell you, but you do not believe. The works I do in my Father's name testify about me (John 10:25).

Anything Jesus did, He did in His Father's name and identity. For Jesus to be One with His Father, He cannot have a separate identity from His Father. The same is true for us. If we are to be One with Jesus or others, we cannot have our own personal identity, which is separate from one another or Jesus.

But what is the name of Jesus' Father? Even scholars have not been able to come to a unanimous conclusion. Yahweh, YHWH, Elohim, God, and Lord are all suggestions. I don't want to get into any intellectual debates. We are here to find what is common to all, rather than how one mind thinks versus another. Please understand that every language will have different words to describe the same name, so we are not here to debate which language is superior. We are here to discover the essence of what is beyond the actual word or name used. The essence of myself is not my actual name any more than Jesus' name is His essence and ever-present Being. Let's look to the passage of Scripture where Moses is at the burning bush and asks the Lord God what His actual name is.

13 Moses said to God, "Suppose I go to the Israelites and say to them, 'The God of your fathers has sent me to you,' and they ask me, 'What is his name?' Then what shall I tell them?"

14 God said to Moses, "I AM WHO I AM. This is what you are to say to the Israelites: 'I AM has sent me to you.'"

15 God also said to Moses, "Say to the Israelites, 'The LORD, the God of your fathers—the God of Abraham, the God of Isaac and the God of Jacob— has sent me to you.'

"This is my name forever, the name you shall call me from generation to generation. (Exodus 3:13-15 NIV)

Perhaps I am reading this passage differently than some expert scholars, but it surely seems as though *I AM* is the name God has always had and will always have. Even though *The LORD* has been thrown into verse 15, I feel as though this is more of a title or role than God's actual name and essence identity. In verse 14, God answers Moses's question directly by saying to tell the Israelites, "'I AM' has sent me to you." A Lord is someone or something that has power over others. The *Someone or Something* that has power over *all* has a name and essence identity of I AM. But when I explain the English name is "I AM," I am not saying another language translation is incorrect. I say all translations are correct. The words "I AM" simply refer to Spirit Being or Divine Being. In any language, the meaning behind the words is the same.

They took palm branches and went out to meet him, shouting, "Hosanna!" "Blessed is he who comes in the name of the Lord!" "Blessed is the king of Israel!" (John 12:13 NIV)

Jesus came in the name or Spirit Being of the One who has power over all creation. Jesus' essence identity was His Spirit Being. Though he walked on the earth in His flesh body, He identified with His Spirit essence (which came from His Father) in everything He said and did. His temporal flesh body and nature were not True and lasting, but His Spirit-nature is True and lasting and how He directly experienced/knew Himself.

[43] I have come in my Father's name, and you do not accept me; but if someone else comes in his own name, you will accept him. [44] How can you believe since you accept glory from one another but do not seek the glory that comes from the only God? (John 5:43-44 NIV)

Jesus is saying He is coming in His Father's I AM Divine Being and Presence. If a person we meet comes in their own separate person identity, we will accept them as a person. Of course, we can't believe in a person's Spirit-nature since we, ourselves, accept the glory that comes from being a temporal person. We do not seek the glory that comes from being eternal Divine Spirit because we are satisfied with this lesser glory of being the temporal person.

"All people are like grass, and all their glory is like the flowers of the field; the grass withers and the flowers fall. (1 Peter 1:24 NIV)

[11] And if what was transitory came with glory, how much greater is the glory of that which lasts! (2 Corinthians 3:11 NIV)

Because the greater glory of that which lasts resides within each temporal person, there is a glory that is naturally present no matter where we go and what we do. However, if we only experience and mentally know ourselves as this temporary entity, we limit our effectiveness.

As we come in the name of Jesus, we must come in Spirit Being. We cannot come as a temporal person with insecurities and personal motives and use the name *Jesus* as though it is a magic word to do and get whatever we please. It doesn't quite work that way, as the sons of Sceva found out.

[13] Some Jews who went around driving out evil spirits tried to invoke the name of the Lord Jesus over those who were demon-possessed. They would say, "In the name of the Jesus whom Paul preaches, I command you to come out." [14] Seven sons of Sceva, a Jewish chief priest, were doing this. [15] One day the evil spirit answered them, "Jesus I know, and Paul I know about, but who are you?" [16] Then the man who had the evil spirit jumped on them and overpowered them all. He gave them such a beating that they ran out of the house naked and bleeding. (Acts 19:13-16 NIV)

As we rest our attention in the center of our hearts, we can know and experience the part of us that is ever-present and has no hidden motive for personal gain. We can ask anything in Jesus' name while we are here. In this central space within ourselves, we are *in* Christ. There is no you *and* Christ. You are *in* Christ, and being within Christ, you *are* Christ, and able to speak in His name and with His authority. This is not a mental activity. We simply abide or put our whole attention into the beingness within the center of our body.

4 Remain in me, as I also remain in you. No branch can bear fruit by itself; it must remain in the vine. Neither can you bear fruit unless you remain in me. (John 15:4 NIV)

Dwell, abide, or remain in the great "I AM." Just as the I AM remains in you (no matter what you may believe or think), remain in this Beingness. Stay here as you read. Stay here as you go about your day. Remain in *I AM*. This *I AM* is here always, wherever you go. It isn't as though your forgetting mentally can somehow change this fact. You exist and *"In Him, we live and move and have our being" (Acts 17:28 NIV)*. We would not live and move and have existence if we were not *in Him* already. **It's not as though we need to do anything to be *in Him*. It is only that we must directly experience this Truth for it to be made real for us.**

Do not be tempted to put on the clothing of your person-self. No one can bear fruit by oneself, as an individual person-being. Remain in this connected beingness in your heart, where you are whole and complete.

11

Who Does the Work?

Looking around my house, I see many devices that plug into the wall and use electricity. Right now, the TV screen in front of me is blank, but a small red light at the bottom of the screen is lit, signifying it has power and is ready to be used. If I were to turn it on, my TV would access channels via the internet or through the antennae. My clock is lit up and tells me what time it is. My refrigerator stays cold. None of these devices can do anything on their own. They all must be plugged in, and when plugged in, they all function in different ways based on their design. Just like electronic devices, I've heard numerous sermon messages that speak of the need for us all to be plugged into the Holy Spirit to have the power of God. And although appliances cannot plug themselves in…somehow, we are expected to plug ourselves in. This is our part. God does His part by supplying the power, and we, as people, must do our part. Not only must we plug ourselves into the Holy Spirit as Christians, but before we can even become Christians, we must take certain steps to become saved from our sin. This is what I've been taught. You, as the reader, may not have been taught these same things, and that is fine. We will look together to see what Scripture says, what science says, and even investigate what our own direct experience says.

First, let's carefully read from the Amplified Classic version of Ephesians 2, which seems to address not only what we could possibly need to be saved from, but also how we can be saved. The "He" in verse 1 seems to refer to God.

¹ *And you [He made alive], when you were dead (slain) by [your] trespasses and sins*

² *In which at one time you walked [habitually]. You were following the course and fashion of this world [were under the sway of the tendency of this present age], following the prince of the power of the air. [You were obedient to and under the control of] the [demon] spirit that still constantly works in the sons of disobedience [the careless, the rebellious, and the unbelieving, who go against the purposes of God].*

³ *Among these we as well as you once lived and conducted ourselves in the passions of our flesh [our behavior governed by our corrupt and sensual nature], obeying the impulses of the flesh and the thoughts of the mind [our cravings dictated by our senses and our dark imaginings]. We were then by nature children of [God's] wrath and heirs of [His] indignation, like the rest of mankind.*

⁴ *But God—so rich is He in His mercy! Because of and in order to satisfy the great and wonderful and intense love with which He loved us,*

⁵ *Even when we were dead (slain) by [our own] shortcomings and trespasses, He made us alive together in fellowship and in union with Christ; [He gave us the very life of Christ Himself, the same new life with which He quickened Him, for] it is by grace (His favor and mercy which you did not deserve) that you are saved (delivered from judgment and made partakers of Christ's salvation).*

⁶ *And He raised us up together with Him and made us sit down together [giving us joint seating with Him] in the heavenly sphere [by virtue of our being] in Christ Jesus (the Messiah, the Anointed One). (Ephesians 2:1-6 AMPC)*

This may be a lot to take in, so I will attempt to draw out certain key points. It would seem that while we are dead to our True Spirit-nature,

God has already made us alive, as well as in union with Christ, giving us the very life of Christ, Himself. In addition, God has given us joint seating with Christ because we are *in* Christ Jesus. We have also been saved and delivered from judgment. We have done absolutely nothing to make this possible. God has done it, and this is the way it is. For it is *even when* we were dead (or have been dead) by our own shortcomings and trespasses that God made us alive and in union with Christ (verse 5).

He is not the God of the dead, but of the living, for to him all are alive. (Luke 20:38 NIV)

From God's perspective, we are all in Christ in our True Spirit-nature. This is what is True and ever-present. Any nature or thing that is temporal is obviously not permanent and, therefore, not True and constant. God stays within what is constant and ever-present and views all events that come and go as a natural phenomenon of the created world.

When we are identified by our temporary flesh nature, we are governed by the *demon spirit* that constantly works in the sons of disobedience, and are, by that nature, children of God's wrath (verse 2). It sounds horrible, but Paul said that both he and the Ephesians were doing this out of habit. Perhaps they had moved on from this at the time of his letter, but they all had experienced this unintentional and habitual identification with their temporal flesh-selves.

For now, let's stick with the message of encouragement God is giving us regarding our True and continual nature, and how we are saved from our temporal nature. Although the Amplified Classic version does a wonderful job of expounding upon everything, I will give you the shorter NIV to make it easier to remember and comprehend.

⁸ For it is by grace you have been saved, through faith—and this is not from yourselves, it is the gift of God— ⁹ not by works, so that no one can boast. ¹⁰ For we are God's handiwork, created in Christ Jesus to do good works, which God prepared in advance for us to do. (Ephesians 2:8-10 NIV)

Despite being mentioned in Ephesians 2:5, Paul felt it important to reiterate in 2:8 that our salvation has absolutely nothing to do with anything we have done, can do, or will do. If we had anything at all to do with it, this would be boasting about something we had said or done to make it so. Our salvation is the gift of God.

Returning to a previous passage in Ephesians 1, it is important to note that our salvation in Christ was preordained and made True before the foundation of the world.

⁴ Even as [in His love] He chose us [actually picked us out for Himself as His own] in Christ before the foundation of the world, that we should be holy (consecrated and set apart for Him) and blameless in His sight, even above reproach, before Him in love. (Ephesians 1:4 AMPC)

The *church* (or called out ones in continual Spiritual assembly) is the Spiritual body mentioned in Ephesians 1:23:

²³ (The church) Which is His body, the fullness of Him Who fills all in all [for in that body lives the full measure of Him Who makes everything complete, and Who fills everything everywhere with Himself].

It is Christ with His ever-present Spirit-nature who fills *everything everywhere* with Himself. I don't know how you feel about this, but for me, this is incredibly great news! In that (Spiritual) Christ body is the *full* measure of Christ, who makes *everything* complete. Christ fills everything, *everywhere* with Himself! From this passage, there doesn't appear to be anything anywhere that is not already filled with the fullness of Christ. The church is just another name for this Spiritual body. Being *called out, set apart,* or *holy* means this ever-present and eternal Spiritual body is completely unchanged by anything temporal or having to do with the world of creation. Every day, we witness people and things being changed and affected by other people and things. So much so that it seems impossible to comprehend anything *not* changing over time. But **here we are, in Christ, as unchanging Spirit, witnessing all this change. It is not actually our core beingness that is changing. From where we see everything happening, like the one behind the camera, we remain set apart from the world of change and impermanence.** If this were not True, the statements in Ephesians 2:5 and 2:8 could not be True.

And one called out to another and said, "Holy, Holy, Holy, is the Lord of hosts, The whole earth is full of His glory." (Isaiah 6:3)

The entire earth cannot be filled with God's glory and also be of something else. If a glass or container is *filled* with something, there is not room in it for anything else. The whole earth is *full* of God's glory. It is not partly filled. Holy is the Lord of hosts. The hosts are the forms on the earth. All forms or things are filled with Christ; otherwise, they wouldn't exist or have life. We, as individual people, are the temples or hosts for the Lord. **The Spiritual glory within all forms is what is True and unchanging. Nothing we can do as temporal people can change God and what is constantly and consistently present.**

Take our sun, for example. The sun always shines. There is nothing we can do to keep the sun from shining. However, the position of the earth can block our view of the sun. We can go into a dark cave or darkened house and no longer see the sun shining. We can even put our hand in front of the sun and no longer see it. Nevertheless, the sun is still there. Just because we are unable to see the sun or directly experience its light does not change anything regarding it. However, the sun is a part of the creation and may someday disappear, whereas Christ, in God, and His Spirit-nature in us is unending.

While we go about our daily activities unaware and blindly ignorant of our ever-present Spirit-Self, we are simply under the sway or influence of the world's habits and tendencies in this present time (Ephesians 2:2). We are ruled by our flesh-nature because we see ourselves as individual people. This is the tendency and habit of the majority of people on earth at this time. Without even knowing it, receiving our identity from all the things we imagine about ourselves or from the things we have done and not done as people, is habitually walking in opposition to God, for He is eternal Spirit. *It is the Spirit who gives life; the flesh profits nothing (John 6:63 NIV).*

To help us understand the point or benefit of being in ignorance of God's presence, I have found Romans 11 to be exceedingly helpful. I am skipping over parts of the chapter to give you the idea without bogging you down with too many details. In this passage, Paul is speaking to the Gentile church at Colossae in answer to the question of what is to become of the Jewish people who have not understood or accepted the message and mystery of Christ. The Gentiles, at the time, were all the people of the world who were not Jews. At the time, the Gentiles were not considered God's chosen people, but God had given Paul the ministry of speaking to the Gentiles to let them know all were accepted by God. Paul explains earlier in his letter to the Colossians in 1:26-27 that this message and mystery has been kept hidden for ages and generations, but it is now made known to those who are ready to hear it. This mystery is: *Christ in you, the hope of glory (Colossians 1:27).* For although Christ had been living within them for ages and generations, the people were not yet ready to comprehend and directly experience His Spiritual presence within themselves. In writing, Paul hopes to shed some light on what is to become of the Jews who do and do not yet comprehend and experience this ever-present mystery.

5 So too at the present time there is a remnant (a small believing minority), selected (chosen) by grace (by God's unmerited favor and graciousness).

6 But if it is by grace (His unmerited favor and graciousness), it is no longer conditioned on works or anything men have done. Otherwise, grace would no longer be grace [it would be meaningless].

7 What then [shall we conclude]? Israel failed to obtain what it sought [God's favor by obedience to the Law]. Only the elect (those chosen few) obtained it, while the rest of them became callously indifferent (blinded, hardened, and made insensible to it).

⁸ As it is written, God gave them a spirit (an attitude) of stupor, eyes that should not see and ears that should not hear, [that has continued] down to this very day....

¹¹ So I ask, Have they stumbled so as to fall [to their utter spiritual ruin, irretrievably]? By no means! But through their false step and transgression salvation [has come] to the Gentiles, so as to arouse Israel [to see and feel what they forfeited] and so to make them jealous....

²⁵ Lest you be self-opinionated (wise in your own conceits), I do not want you to miss this hidden truth and mystery, brethren: a hardening (insensibility) has [temporarily] befallen a part of Israel [to last] until the full number of the ingathering of the Gentiles has come in,

²⁶ And so all Israel will be saved. As it is written, The Deliverer will come from Zion, He will banish ungodliness from Jacob.

²⁷ And this will be My covenant (My agreement) with them when I shall take away their sins.

²⁸ From the point of view of the Gospel (good news), they [the Jews, at present] are enemies [of God], which is for your advantage and benefit. But from the point of view of God's choice (of election, of divine selection), they are still the beloved (dear to Him) for the sake of their forefathers....

³⁰ Just as you were once disobedient and rebellious toward God but now have obtained [His] mercy, through their disobedience,

³¹ So they also now are being disobedient [when you are receiving mercy], that they in turn may one day, through the mercy you are enjoying, also receive mercy [that they may share the mercy which has been shown to you—through you as messengers of the Gospel to them].

³² For God has consigned (penned up) all men to disobedience, only that He may have mercy on them all [alike].

³³ Oh, the depth of the riches and wisdom and knowledge of God! How unfathomable (inscrutable, unsearchable) are His judgments (His decisions)! And how untraceable (mysterious, undiscoverable) are His ways (His methods, His paths)!

[34] For who has known the mind of the Lord and who has understood His thoughts, or who has [ever] been His counselor?

[35] Or who has first given God anything that he might be paid back or that he could claim a recompense?

[36] For from Him and through Him and to Him are all things. [For all things originate with Him and come from Him; all things live through Him, and all things center in and tend to consummate and to end in Him.] To Him be glory forever! Amen (so be it). (Romans 11: 5-8, 11, 25-28, 30-36 AMPC)

"Is this really God's plan for salvation?" you ask. Let's quickly review the main points above.

1. God has made us all Spiritually one in Christ because we are His Spiritual offspring.

2. Some have accepted and discovered this oneness in the center of their being, and live experientially from this place.

3. Many have not discovered this Truth, or have heard about it, but not internalized it to where it can be experienced.

4. God has intentionally blinded and made deaf those who have not yet understood and discovered the ever-present Truth inside them.

5. God has allowed all humankind to experience a feeling of separation and distance from Christ in order that He can then shower all of them with His love and mercy when they find Him again. (It is the story of the prodigal son.)

6. As we rediscover what is constant and True within ourselves (Christ), we become messengers of the good news.

7. In verse 36 is found the super-good, exceedingly great news, that all things (or people) originate with Christ, come from Christ, live through His beingness and power (grace), center in, come together in unity, and end in Him.

I am not making this stuff up! Read it for yourselves. This is all amazing news! God's prevenient grace, or His wonder-working power, is at work within us all before we even know it is there. And as we begin to directly experience God's grace, it continues to work within us, at all times.

Anything that we do is powered by God. Even our disobedience or failure to recognize His Spirit living within us has a place in the grand scheme.

God chose you as firstfruits to be saved through the sanctifying work of the Spirit and through belief in the truth. (2 Thessalonians 2:13 NIV)

The sanctifying work of the Spirit is what saves us. And His Spirit, ever-present within us, which is Truth, opens our eyes to His Presence, which, in turn, heals our temporary blindness.

They perish because they refused to love the truth and so be saved. (2 Thessalonians 2:10 NIV)

If I tell you I have black chairs in my kitchen, you have a choice whether to believe I am telling you a true story. You have no way of knowing if I am a reliable source. I could be telling you the truth, or perhaps not. You will need to decide somehow. But I *know* I have black chairs in my kitchen. I see them and experience them every time I am in the kitchen. I do not need to believe I have black chairs in my kitchen. It is true for me because I directly experience them. Beliefs can change based on what is intellectually known or what is directly experienced over time in our flesh bodies. If you are one of the people who have not seen or directly experienced that I have black chairs in my kitchen, but you believe what I've told you, you can add that belief to your list of personal accomplishments. Your person-self has believed. If you don't believe what I've told you, your person-self can also claim this victory and position of *not* believing. In reading the following passage, in which Paul and Silas were questioned on what must be done to be saved, the answer seems to point to some kind of direct experience and knowingness, like how I know I have black chairs in my kitchen, rather than a mentally constructed belief and effort, which could be claimed as something they had done and accomplished.

30 He then brought them out and asked, "Sirs, what must I do to be saved?"

31 They replied, "Believe in the Lord Jesus, and you will be saved—you and your household." (Acts 16:30-31)

If a mental belief were required, we would need to come upon some kind of information and knowledge about Jesus. Someone would need to tell us about Jesus, or we would need to read about Him. And even after receiving all of this information, we still only know about Jesus conceptually, or as an idea. We may spend the rest of our lives devoted to finding information about everything Jesus said and did, but this is still not the same as knowing Him experientially. As we discussed earlier, I may have a can of jackfruit in my pantry, but until I experience it, I only mentally know everything about jackfruit and what it might taste like and do for me.

The instructions for believing in the Lord Jesus in Acts 16:31 seem a bit vague to me. What exactly do we need to believe? Do we just need to believe Jesus existed? Must we believe He was God's Son? Must we believe He was raised from the dead? And why would Acts 16:31 only tell us part of the requirements if more are involved?

I wonder how anyone can be made to believe anything, even if they want to. I can tell you many things all about Jesus and the wonderful and divine things He did while on the earth as God in flesh. But in this situation, you still have to make a judgment in deciding whether to believe all that I tell you. Perhaps I am not trustworthy. What if you are convinced while I am standing before you, but tomorrow you aren't so sure about the truth of what I've said? In order for there to be no wavering of belief, depending on how you are feeling about me or my words, you will need evidence in the way of some real tangible experience. Often, the word "belief" in Scripture is actually speaking of a deep trust due to an experiential knowing within Spirit, and within the center of one's being. Here, in the center of your beingness, your belief is coming *from* the Lord Jesus. You are *in* Jesus, and in Christ, and it is this direct experience of being here right now in the Lord Jesus that makes your belief real and unwavering. From this perspective, *Believe in the Lord Jesus* means your trust and confidence *comes from* the place of the Lord Jesus (which is your ever-present Spirit-beingness). This belief and trust *coming from* the Lord Jesus, in the center of your being, has an entirely different feeling and effect than being told I should mentally believe in something I have no direct experience of.

If my husband tells me he will meet me at Walgreens today at 1:45, I know he intends to do that and hopes to do that. I believe he will be there, but until he is actually there at 1:45, I can't really know for certain. It turns out he was at Walgreens at 1:47. So in actuality, he was not there at 1:45, even though I believed he would be. If my husband had been at Walgreens at 1:45, it would only be then, when I could know and speak with confidence about his presence at Walgreens at 1:45. It would no longer be a mental belief, but an actual knowing based in directly experiencing his presence. That my husband was actually *not* at Walgreens at 1:45 further proves the point that people can be untrustworthy and not consistently True, even though they mean well. What *is* consistently True is Christ living within them, whether or not they or you are aware of it.

⁴ Remain in me, as I also remain in you. No branch can bear fruit by itself; it must remain in the vine. Neither can you bear fruit unless you remain in me. (John 15:4 NIV)

Christ remains in us within the center of our being. He is not claiming a separate existence apart from us. While we use our human minds to form an image of who we are as an individual temporary flesh person, we are simultaneously creating an imagined separation between Christ and us. There is now a duality, where in Truth, we are one. In Spirit and unchangeable Truth, we are together, where there is no male or female or difference created by physical or imagined distinction.

Exhibiting the fruit of the Spirit—*love, joy, peace, patience, kindness, goodness, faithfulness, gentleness, and self-control (Galatians 5:22-23 NIV)*—occurs while we are in our Spirit-beingness, rather than operating out of an individual person-self. Remaining *in* the vine, we cannot also be separate from the vine. In ever-present Truth, we could never be separate from the vine, for *in Him, we live, and move, and have our being (Acts 17:28)*. But we can imagine ourselves as separate people very easily, believing truth to be what we see in the temporary, continually changing created world.

Once again, *They perish because they refused to love the truth and so be saved. (2 Thessalonians 2:10 NIV)*

If the Truth were something temporary, or a story someone tells that we must ascertain, whether or not it happened and is real, how could we know with any certainty? Everyone witnessing a scene will have a different perspective and takeaway. What is witnessed is true from that place. However, if this truth is not consistent between all witnesses, there will *always* be discrepancy and disagreement. To find the Truth that does *not* cause discrepancy and disagreement (which is the Truth we must love, and so be saved), we will need to look beyond anything that can be claimed as specific to any one person, religion, or belief. We cannot even look to what is specific to *my* beliefs. Anything I speak of must be True and consistent for you, as well.

Remind yourself of Romans 11 where Paul explains it is God who has given men an attitude of stupor and bound *all* men to disobedience, only that He may have mercy on them all.

Quite honestly, it was not until I experienced the loss of what I treasured and held so very dear to me that I even became open enough to find true healing. I found myself in so much emotional pain that I could not continue in that condition. I did not want to live anymore. I could not see the point. Nothing brought me joy, and I could not feel thankfulness for anything. I saw every experience filtered through a state of sorrow, disappointment, and pessimism. I had put my entire heart and livelihood into being the best me I could be, loving, and continually forgiving my friend for everything that seemed hurtful to me. I had done everything I had known to do to show my love and caring for her, but she had rejected me fully. All my efforts were not good enough. She had experienced enough of me and didn't want to see or hear from me anymore, even though I had thought I had been the best me I could be. What more could I be or do?

It was from this bottom-of-the-pit experience that I finally began to ask and seek out what truth was. My friend had told me she loved and cared about me, but it sure didn't feel like it at the time. Though my friend had experienced a *hardening of the heart*, it was all so I might discover a truth and love that does not come and go like the wind. Like with the Jews referenced in Romans 11, a temporary hardness of heart had occurred so I could be set free from my life of bondage. I had been trusting in things that come and go. I had been working so hard to find approval and acceptance from others when I didn't feel approval and acceptance from within. I was trying so hard to find ministries and accomplishments to add to my personal resume, in hopes of feeling better about my self-image. I was enslaved to the ways of the world without even knowing it! I thought I was devoting myself to God, and doing all the right Christian things. But if I had been honest with myself, I was miserable even before the great rejection and separation from my friend.

I believed in God. I believed Jesus was God's Son in the flesh. I believed Jesus had died and was resurrected and had saved me from my sin. I woke up early and devoted the firstfruits of my day to God, and I did my best to be surrendered to whatever might be asked of me. But in all honesty, I was caught up in being tossed to-and-fro like the waves of the sea. When things were going as I wanted, I was high on life, but as soon as difficulties and perceived rejection arose, I sank lowly into disappointment and depression from that former high. Even though I was confident of my salvation as it had been explained to me, that confidence did not truly help me feel continually free. I did not live out of abundance, but out of lack and not enough. I would sing on the praise team at church, and love it, but the voice of criticism would haunt me afterwards. I would write letters of appreciation to my friends, but then wonder if those letters were well-received. I would give gifts of baked bread and countless other things to a great many people. Some would never even say anything about having received those gifts, so I would concern myself over whether they were appreciated.

Without even being aware, I was simply living from my temporal person-self. Most of the world does this, so we don't really think anything of it. But if it hadn't been for the perceived rejection and unkindness of others, I would not have sought out a way to find stability in something that does not change or come and go. Even my ideas about God and His feelings toward me changed based on how I felt about my personal self.

Though it makes no logical sense to the mind of man, we all must go through a prodigal son experience, where we feel the harshness of the world which is living in separation from Christ and His continual love and acceptance. Even Jesus Christ was sent into the wilderness to be tempted by the devil (suggestions of the mind) that He could somehow benefit as a Spiritual Being by having the power (or food) of the temporal world. **The world is not actually here so it can conform to your personal wishes and desires, but to help you find your comfort and peace apart from it, and in spite of how the world appears.**

Similar to religious teachings, science is now discovering what we hold in common, which saves us from the sin and separated state of the created world. Different words may be used, but it is speaking of the same unseen principle at work within the created world.

In Chapter 9 on the Word of God, I mentioned the ability to scientifically measure heart-brain coherence. When we have a high level of heart-brain coherence, our whole body functions more effectively, we are able to make more intuitive decisions, and we have more beneficial emotions and brain function. HeartMath Institute markets an inner balance sensor designed to help us find higher levels of heart-brain coherence. Many smartwatches are now designed to measure stress levels and even alert us when we could benefit from some deep breathing. Although stress can help us quickly get out of some dangerous situations, our bodies don't function efficiently under the continual influence of a flood of stress hormones. But even stress hormones are playing an important role in motivating us to find God and what is faithfully stable within us. The feeling we have when in higher levels of heart-brain coherence is that of an inner calmness. If we continually have, and use this inner calmness, as we face life situations, we are essentially *saved* from the continually changing ups and downs and fears of the world.

Place your attention in the center of your body and simply breathe from here for a while. Say *thank you* one time, or repeatedly, and rest in this feeling of thankfulness. While you rest here, you are not creating this space. This space is always here, and you are simply resting in it. Thoughts may come, but you are still resting in your heart, and in your beingness, where Christ lives.

For in the day of trouble he will keep me safe in his dwelling; he will hide me in the shelter of his sacred tent and set me high upon a rock. (Psalm 27:5 NIV)

12

The Only Thing That Counts

Both my husband and I jumped up in bed at the same time. I realized it was 2 a.m. and my cell phone was ringing. As soon as I remembered who I was and where I was, I answered my phone.

"John finally has a job, but the person who has been giving him a ride to work can't do it anymore, and he has no way to get to work at 7 a.m. this morning and for the rest of the week. Do you think you or Karl could give him a ride to and from work this week? We don't know what else to do! John needs this job so we can pay the rent," my friend Chrissy said.

Quickly, my mind raced through all the possible scenarios. Too many other things were happening in our lives for us to commit to driving John to and from work for a week. But just a week ago, we had bought a third used car to replace the twenty-year-old car we owned. We couldn't possibly loan out our oldest car. It had no air conditioning or heat, starting it was tricky since the key no longer worked in the ignition, and it was prone to overheating. There were just too many quirky things with it to explain to someone else. I would be needing the minivan to take my kids where they needed to go that week, as well as to drive Chrissy and her children where they needed to go while John was at work. The only car we could possibly loan out was the newer one we had just gotten. This solution just felt right to me.

"Hold on for a minute, Chrissy. Let me talk to Karl," I said. I put my phone on mute, turned to Karl, and explained the situation and what we could do to help. "If we drive the car over right now, since we are already awake, John could have it in time to be at work at 7 a.m.," I heard myself saying. Karl was groggy but adamant that he didn't want to loan our nicest car out to anyone.

"We'll never get our car back! The answer is no!" he exploded.

I was strangely calm inside. "What else can we do? I think it is our best and only real option," I said. I knew it was what we should do, but my husband was not convinced.

"I just want to go back to bed, and pretend we never got a phone call," he said as he put his head back on his pillow and pulled up the bed covers.

Honestly, I wanted to do the same thing. It was the middle of the night, and I was tired. I could hear all of my mind's reasonings, but I also had a strong feeling and conviction that we should loan our car to my friend's husband so he could work for the next week. I did not have any fears our car wouldn't be returned. It felt *right*. I felt whole and complete and confidently supported within. Maybe you could say I had faith. **It wasn't as much a faith in something as it was a confidence coming from well-being.** After my husband became more awake, he must have come to the same inner faith because we ended up driving our newest and best car over to my friend's house.

Since the word *faith* is used extensively throughout the Scriptures, it is crucial we have a clear understanding of what it actually means. Hebrews 11:1 gives us some clues.

Now faith is confidence in what we hope for and assurance about what we do not see. (NIV)

Rather than being a blind trust, faith is more of a confidence and assurance. The Amplified Bible adds that it is a conviction of the reality of something not seen or revealed to the senses. If I tell you anything at all, you can't truly have an unwavering conviction of its reality unless you also experience, or have experienced, this same reality for yourself. If I tell you eating my homemade bread with freshly milled whole wheat flour will make you feel better and help to make your body stronger and healthier, you cannot have an unwavering faith in my bread to accomplish all that I say without any evidence. If I tell you stories about how other people have been healed of many ailments from eating my bread, you could be more convinced. But it is fair to say you still might have some doubts.

As Jesus walked the earth and went from town to town, He was quoted as noticing *little faith, great faith,* or faith that had brought healing to a person. He spoke often of how faith without doubt could accomplish many things. Romans 12:3 tells us each person has been given a measure of faith. So even when Jesus mentions a lack of faith, He must mean the person has faith, but is not currently acting as though they have it.

In Acts 3, Peter and John encountered a man lame from birth who was brought daily to beg at the temple gate called Beautiful. Peter healed the man in the name of Jesus, and the onlookers were amazed.

By faith in the name of Jesus, this man whom you see and know was made strong. It is Jesus' name and the faith that comes through him that has completely healed him, as you can all see. (Acts 3:16 NIV)

The faith Peter exhibited was in the *name of Jesus,* which we discussed earlier as being more than simply the word "Jesus." Other languages use other names for Jesus. And Jesus, Himself, said He came in the name of His Father, which is "I AM." The word *Jesus* can be used, but it is the beingness supporting the word that gives the word its power and strength. For it was the Name (or Spirit-beingness) and the faith that comes through Christ that had completely healed the man. Peter did not claim that he, as a person, had done any healing. It was Christ (Spirit) within Peter, and within the man born lame, that accomplished the healing.

Before Paul was entrusted with the message of faith for the Gentiles, the religious Pharisees and many others were confused about what was required of them not only to be saved, but also to be justified and sanctified by God. Today, many of us are still confused about these same issues.

30 What then shall we say? That the Gentiles, who did not pursue righteousness, have obtained it, a righteousness that is by faith; 31 but the people of Israel, who pursued the law as the way of righteousness, have not attained their goal. 32 Why not? Because they pursued it not by faith but as if it were by works. They stumbled over the stumbling stone. (Romans 9:30-32 NIV)

The people of Israel were given the Law of Moses back in the day when they preferred not to meet with God, and instead asked for Moses to be their intercessor. The only True way of becoming saved or sanctified is to meet in Spirit with God, who is Spirit, but the Israelites wanted a work-around. They preferred to know what they must do to be saved.

18 Now all the people perceived the thunderings and the lightnings and the noise of the trumpet and the smoking mountain, and as [they] looked they trembled with fear and fell back and stood afar off.

19 And they said to Moses, You speak to us and we will listen, but let not God speak to us, lest we die.

20 And Moses said to the people, Fear not; for God has come to prove you, so that the [reverential] fear of Him may be before you, that you may not sin. (Exodus 20:18-20 AMPC)

The proving of *you* that Moses spoke of refers to our True Spirit-beingness. God has come to prove the Truth of His steadfast Spirit alive and well within us all. As we keep our eyes fixed on Christ, it is His I AMness that pervades our consciousness and is *before* us, as a person. (*Looking unto Jesus, the author and finisher of our faith. Hebrews 12:2 NKJV*) **From the center of our being and I AMness, we are fixed on Christ, and it is from here that our faith comes alive and is perfected.**

As Christ's Spirit-nature in us becomes greater, our flesh identity becomes less. (*You, dear children, are from God and have overcome them, because the one who is in you is greater than the one who is in the world. 1 John 4:4 NIV*) The one who is in the world is the flesh body and (flesh) mind-generated concept of ourselves. This is the *one doomed to destruction*. All of creation is subject to decay and eventual destruction. We are *not* subject to decay, as Spirit-beings. This is our ever-present Reality, and the One we temporarily lose sight of, as we buy into our mind-generated ideas about who we are.

Our continual Spirit-beingness can only be directly experienced. Me telling you that you are a Spirit being doesn't make it real for you. It is True and ever-present, but if your Spirit-being is dominated by your mind's conceptualization of it, this reality remains an idea in the head. Your Spirit-beingness, as an idea, can be pointed to, as something separate from you, and something to be grasped or attained. **Spirit-beingness becomes a *stumbling stone* when it remains an idea or concept apart from ourselves. As a concept, idea, or thing, it is separate from us and a destination and goal to be worked toward, and then finally attained.**

Spirit is the essence of who we are, and as such, must be directly experienced, and known as us, without any separation of ideas. The issue is that we can't work toward an idea of who we Truly are and finally get there. If we are at our house, no amount of thinking about how to get to our house will help us to arrive there. We are already home, and all we can do is experience being home to know it is real. We can look at pictures of our home and imagine what it is like to be there. We can read all about our home and what other people think about our home, but only living there can eliminate the separation created in the mind between the idea of our home and the reality of our home. Living there is the reality, but thinking about it or attempting to get there will never create its reality. Mentally knowing of our Spirit-beingness and directly experiencing the beingness are somewhat analogous to knowing about our home and directly experiencing our home.

During their exodus from Egypt, the Israelites were afraid to have God speak to them after they saw Him cover the mountain in fire and smoke. The fire is symbolic of God's purifying and proving of us, as gold is proved and made pure in the fire. The only thing left after the purification is our True and ever-present Spirit-beingness in Christ. There is no longer us *and* Christ, but just us, as Christ, in our Spirit-Selves. If we are *in* Christ, we are not separate from Christ, but in Him and a part of Him.

Although we may come to know of our salvation in Christ, it is often a mental knowing, rather than directly experiencing oneness in Christ, as our Spirit-Selves. Because we are still living predominantly from our flesh-mind's control and dominance, we cannot comprehend how our unkind thoughts and actions can be acceptable or completely forgiven by God. We cannot forget and let go of our past errors. The people around us can't seem to forget and let the past remain in the past, either. We continually mentally compare ourselves to Christ and discern the gap or difference between Him and us. This creates a need to perfect our actions so we can be more like Christ. **Our human minds keep looking to the mentally created gap between us and Christ, rather than actually meeting with Christ in His Presence within the center of our being. This heart-center is where our faith is made alive and perfected.**

The people of Israel were also caught up in this flesh-mind dominated living and tried to perfect their behavior based on following the guidelines or Law of Moses. They would not and could not come to oneness with God by this method, and neither can we. Jesus told the Jewish leaders, *"Do not think I will accuse you before the Father. Your accuser is Moses, on whom your hopes are set" (John 5:45 NIV)*. Moses, in this verse, represents the flesh-mind attempting to earn righteousness and right-standing with God by following the Law.

Abraham, on the other hand, is credited with being the father of faith, through which salvation comes.

¹ What then shall we say that Abraham, our forefather according to the flesh, discovered in this matter? ² If, in fact, Abraham was justified by works, he had something to boast about—but not before God. ³ What does Scripture say? "Abraham believed God, and it was credited to him as righteousness."

⁴ Now to the one who works, wages are not credited as a gift but as an obligation. ⁵ However, to the one who does not work but trusts God who justifies the ungodly, their faith is credited as righteousness. (Romans 4:1-5 NIV)

Not only did Abraham *believe* God, but his conviction of absolute, unchanging truth came *from* God. His conviction, or his unwavering stability in God/Christ/his Spirit-Self, was credited to him as righteousness. His remaining in the reality of the Spirit-nature within the center of his being is what made it possible for him to be righteous. The righteousness of God is attainable only through resting in Christ's Being and Reality within our heart-center. Our person-self is not eternal and cannot earn salvation. We can only find salvation within Spirit and through the work of Spirit. Knowing all this mentally may help, but it is no substitute for directly experiencing and living from this True place of stability.

As Romans 4:1-5 says above, it is God who justifies the ungodly. It is His Beingness and acceptance without judgment that cleanses and purifies our critical and condemning flesh-mind, which sees the mental separation between *us* and *God* and keeps judging our shortcomings, as well as those in the world.

For everyone born of God overcomes the world. This is the victory that has overcome the world, even our faith. (1 John 5:4 NIV)

The only ones born of God are Spirit, for *Spirit gives birth to Spirit and flesh gives birth to flesh (John 6:3 NIV)*. Once again, our temporal flesh-selves cannot overcome the world because as flesh persons, we are a part of the temporary created world. Only within the reality of our ever-present Spirit-beingness can we know our stability and lasting nature beyond that of our flesh and mentally created ideas that come and go within our beingness.

[15] *"We who are Jews by birth and not sinful Gentiles* [16] *know that a person is not justified by the works of the law, but by faith in Jesus Christ. So we, too, have put our faith in Christ Jesus that we may be justified by faith in Christ and not by the works of the law, because by the works of the law no one will be justified. (Galatians 3:16 NIV)*

I have been crucified with Christ and I no longer live, but Christ lives in me. (Galatians 3:20 NIV)

Paul has been crucified and no longer lives as Paul, who has a separate identity from Christ. It is the Spirit-nature of Christ that is now predominant within the body of Paul. Paul says it is not *I*, Paul, who is alive, but Christ. Paul's personal flesh identity is *dead* and actually never had *eternal* and ever-present Life.

Jesus also spoke to us about the need to deny our temporal and personal-self.

[24] *Then Jesus said to his disciples, "Whoever wants to be my disciple must deny themselves and take up their cross and follow me.* [25] *For whoever wants to save their life will lose it, but whoever loses their life for me will find it.* [26] *What good will it be for someone to gain the whole world, yet forfeit their soul? (Matthew 16: 24-26 NIV)*

To deny is to declare something to be untrue, according to Merriam-Webster.com. And to deny ourselves quite simply means to know our flesh bodies and minds as not *True* or constant. Yes, this flesh mind and body exist for a time, but they had a birth and will have a death. They are not always and consistently True and ever-present. It is not who we are, and Jesus wants us to take up our cross *daily*, die to our personal nature, and live from our Spiritual nature and reality, which is *True* and constant. Whoever wants to save their personal-self will end up losing it. Not only does the personal-self die a physical death, but it is also continually changing. Our physical bodies mostly regenerate at the cellular level every 7-10 years. So the bodies we have today are not the same as they were yesterday. The thoughts we experience right now are not the same thoughts that presented themselves even an hour ago. As we discover Christ, and our ever-present Being, we lose our personalized life and who we are individually, apart from Christ. Jesus asks us what good will it be to gain a temporal perspective and temporary sense of security at the expense of losing the essence of who we are? The created world is only here for a time and then ends. The *"self"* that Jesus tells us we should deny is the idea of who we are apart from Him, which only has a temporary existence for as long as we buy into it.

Paul's message throughout Scripture asserts that no person can be justified by anything done in the body of flesh. It is our faith coming from beingness *in Christ* or in I AMness that justifies, forgives, and gives us peace in God. If we can claim *we* have faith or *attained faith*, there is a personal identity boasting about something that has been done to attain faith or salvation. We are boasting in *our* correct beliefs and choices of what we believe and trust in, which have *earned* our salvation.

Paul said, *"My message and my preaching were not with wise and persuasive words, but with a demonstration of the Spirit's power,⁵ so that your faith might not rest on human wisdom, but on God's power." (1 Corinthians 2:5 NIV)*

Paul was trying to convey that the message he delivered, as well as the message's ability to be received by those who heard it, was in no way dependent upon the wisdom of the flesh. Both the delivery of the message and its comprehension were a demonstration of God's power, and God's power, alone.

The sabbath rest for man is meant to be symbolic of the rest from our striving to attain righteousness and goodness through our temporal flesh-selves.

[F]or anyone who enters God's rest also rests from their works, just as God did from his. (Hebrews 4:10 NIV)

On the seventh day, God rested from creating and achieving. In order to rest or abide in God, we must do likewise. In the story in Luke 10:38-42 about Martha and Mary, Jesus explains about resting in Being.

38 As Jesus and his disciples were on their way, he came to a village where a woman named Martha opened her home to him. 39 She had a sister called Mary, who sat at the Lord's feet listening to what he said. 40 But Martha was distracted by all the preparations that had to be made. She came to him and asked, "Lord, don't you care that my sister has left me to do the work by myself? Tell her to help me!"

41 "Martha, Martha," the Lord answered, "you are worried and upset about many things, 42 but few things are needed—or indeed only one. Mary has chosen what is better, and it will not be taken away from her." (NIV)

Although serving others has its place, it will come out of being in communion with Christ, within our beingness. Jesus says it is this beingness that cannot be taken from Mary…or us. We can lose everything we cherish most in the world, but the essence of our beingness cannot disappear or be taken from us, ever. In the story, Mary had met with Jesus in person, but his flesh body was taken from her, both when He left Martha's home, as well as more permanently when He was crucified. When explaining what one thing is needed, and can never be taken from us, He meant His Spirit, the I AMness within, and the Spirit that gives all humankind ever-present and eternal Life in the here and now, and forever-after.

The Ten Commandments exist to help govern those living under the control of the temporal flesh-mind. As we live from *Being*, the personal self and its fears, insecurities, and sinful nature of our flesh-mind do not control our actions. From our place of stability and faith, or our Christ-center, we instinctively do what is right.

[23] Before the coming of this faith, we were held in custody under the law, locked up until the faith that was to come would be revealed. [24] So the law was our guardian until Christ came that we might be justified by faith. [25] Now that this faith has come, we are no longer under a guardian.

[26] So in Christ Jesus you are all children of God through faith, [27] for all of you who were baptized into Christ have clothed yourselves with Christ. [28] There is neither Jew nor Gentile, neither slave nor free, nor is there male and female, for you are all one in Christ Jesus. [29] If you belong to Christ, then you are Abraham's seed, and heirs according to the promise. (Galatians 3:23-29 NIV)

We are *all* one in Christ Jesus in Spirit. As people dominated by our flesh-minds, all we see are differences caused by gender or religious belief or lack of belief. This is the separation caused by the temporal flesh-mind. In Christ, and *clothed with Christ*, we can see physical difference or behavior differences. However, because there is no judgment or separation happening within the center of our being, in I AMness we find our oneness or unity.

[4] You who are trying to be justified by the law have been alienated from Christ; you have fallen away from grace. [5] For through the Spirit we eagerly await by faith the righteousness for which we hope. (Galatians 5:4-5 NIV)

I did not know I was trying to be justified by the Law or by my flesh mind. I thought I was just trying to do all the right Christian things to become closer to God. Although I got up early to *be with God*, I was hoping that reading Scriptures daily would make me more like Christ. I trusted that memorization of Scripture would somehow transform my temporary flesh-mind to be like the mind of Christ. I believed daily speaking with God would make me closer to Him. I put my trust in my Christian actions or *works* to become sanctified by God. This is what my flesh-mind was doing. I saw a separation between how I was and how I wanted to be, which was more like Christ. I held an image in my mind of how I should be and used Christian teaching and philosophy to guide me in all I should do to be more like Christ. I did not know just *being* was all that was needed or that it could never be taken from me. I misunderstood the message of good news, *Christ in you, the hope of glory* (Colossians 1:27). I thought I had to do something to somehow generate a more stable faith within myself. When people put me down and turned against me, I felt as though my faith crumbled simultaneously. I no longer had a strong belief that God had a good plan for me or my life. My mind criticized me for my lack of faith, and I felt defective. Once again, I would need to *do* something to find my way back to God. There was a *me* and *God*, or a *me* and *Christ*. There was a *me* trying to do things to hopefully and eventually become more Christ-like.

Paul explained that when we are trying to be justified by the Law, or by what we do or don't do, we are alienated from our Christ-center and beingness. We are overtaken by the reasonings and thoughts of the flesh-mind, causing us to see comparisons between one thing and another. We can never find unity in Christ when we are trying to use our minds to get there. It will always be an idea separate from who we are. The righteousness you and I seek is within us. It is found in Beingness and in the stability of this faithful and unchanging heart-center. *For through the Spirit, we eagerly await by faith (strong conviction found from directly experiencing Christ), the righteousness for which we hope (Galatians 5:5).* **It is the work of Christ's nature within us that brings about our divinely righteous acts.** If our righteousness comes from something we have said, done, or accomplished, as an individual person, it comes from works. Instead…

²² let us draw near to God with a sincere heart and with the full assurance that faith brings, having our hearts sprinkled to cleanse us from a guilty conscience and having our bodies washed with pure water. (Hebrews 10:22)

We draw near to God with an honest and True heart-center—the part of us that is ever-present, rather than here today and gone tomorrow. Our heart-center cleanses us from a guilty conscience. It isn't the right actions we do, or the lack of wrong actions as a person, that cleanse us from a guilty conscience. It is viewing our personal actions from our True self, which helps us to realize this person-self is not us, if we can watch it and observe it.

Paul describes this false flesh-self as *"sin"* or *"sin principle."*

Now if I do what I do not want to do, it is no longer I who do it, but it is sin living in me that does it. (Romans 7:20 NIV)

What Paul is attempting to convey is: There is an *i* who does what his I (In Christ) does not want to do. This *i* who does what his Spirit-nature opposes is not Truly himself. It is the sin-principle, false-self, or old-personal temporal self apart from Christ. As we are able to view this temporal self from the place of our True and ever-present self, we realize its impermanence and unreality. Our placement within Christ, in the center of our being, is prominent and aware of what is appearing within us as impermanent.

In asking how our faith can transform our behavior, Paul explains that Christ equips His people for works of service. It doesn't matter what role we may play, it is all Christ within us who enables us to do good works and spread the message of His great love and power living within all humankind without exception. *For God does not show favoritism (Romans 2:11 NIV).* God is omnipresent, and there is no place He is not.

⁷ But to each one of us grace has been given as Christ apportioned it. ⁸ This is why it says:

*"When he ascended on high,
  he took many captives
  and gave gifts to his people."*

⁹ (What does "he ascended" mean except that he also descended to the lower, earthly regions? ¹⁰ He who descended is the very one who ascended higher than all the heavens, in order to fill the whole universe.) ¹¹ So Christ himself gave the apostles, the prophets, the evangelists, the pastors and teachers, ¹² to equip his people for works of service, so that the body of Christ may be built up ¹³ until we all reach unity in the faith and in the knowledge of the Son of God and become mature, attaining to the whole measure of the fullness of Christ. (Ephesians 4:7-13)

I memorized all of Ephesians years ago, and I recited it daily, but I had no idea of the full implications of these verses. Christ is using us all, even in our sin, to build up the Spiritual body of Christ. According to the Scripture passage above, there is a time when we will all reach unity in the faith. If we all had to come to some kind of mental agreement about what we should all believe or what is true versus false, unity could never be possible. Those who are mentally challenged, or the very young who have not even learned human language, could not be included. No, this unity in the faith that Paul speaks of is one reached through directly experiencing Christ. Mentally knowing about Christ does not help us to reach more than a superficial and temporary unity, and it excludes those who do not have the mental capacity to process information. Directly experiencing the Trueness of our impartial heart-center, on the other hand, is how we can all find unity and the whole measure of the fullness of Christ. It is something we all have, and it is not something we need to do or earn. **Our flesh minds and individual conditioning will always keep us separated by ideas and concepts. But only one thing is needed, which can never be taken from us, and it is the essence of our being.**

13

What About Hell, the Lake of Fire, the Sheep and the Goats, and the Man of Lawlessness?

The night before last, I watched the movie *The Best Exotic Marigold Hotel*. One of the main characters had returned to India after being away for forty years. At the time he had left India, his treasured male friend and that friend's entire family had been banished by his community after it was discovered the main character and his male friend had been in a homosexual relationship. This main character hadn't known what to do to help the situation, so he had left India. During those forty years, the main character had tormented himself, believing he was at fault for destining his friend to a life of trouble. After much trepidation, the main character called upon his friend forty years later, only to find out his friend had been quite content. He was happily married to a woman and had shared with his wife all about his on-going love for the main character. The husband and wife had no secrets from each other and were living a fulfilled life. Relieved, the main character felt a huge burden lifted from him. All those years, he had imagined his friend might be angry with him for abandoning him, and he had pictured his friend living out the rest of his years in misery because of his discovered homosexuality. None of what he had imagined had been true, and as he was freed from those thoughts, he felt as though he had been released from a type of prison.

Have you, also, been released from any type of misunderstanding of the past? My youngest daughter, Amy, began nursing school this year, in addition to working overnight shifts at the hospital full-time, plus caring for her two young children. I imagine myself, if I were in the same situation, being overwhelmed, continually tired, and unable to cope. On the days Amy must go directly from work to class for six hours, and then get only a few hours of rest before going back to work overnight, I picture her dragging herself from one place to another. However, when I talk to her afterward, she tells me it wasn't so bad. Why would I sacrifice my own well-being and sanity when she wasn't actually going through these imagined things? And even if she were, how would my sacrifice benefit her? Why do we imagine these worst-case scenarios when we really don't know? And how does it benefit others to suffer and feel miserable along with them, in challenging situations?

How many times have we thought or imagined the reason someone said or didn't say something, only later to find out it wasn't the case at all? When my pastor friend hadn't been able to commit to spending time together, I assumed it was *me*. Something about *me* wasn't fun enough or just enough. That is what I believed anyway. She had told me how busy and overwhelmed she was, but for some reason, I imagined those were just excuses to cover up her lack of interest in me because of my own shortcomings. It never occurred to me that she really was so overwhelmed that she couldn't add one more thing to her calendar or just needed a little down time to recuperate whenever she could get it. I took it personally because I had a lengthy track record of finding and then losing friends for unexplained reasons. Yes, I may have said or done something (sometimes unknown to me) that may have been the last straw for others, but now I realize it wasn't *just* me.

For some reason, I went around assuming everyone else was more put-together and stable than me. I arrogantly thought I was completely to blame and, therefore, defective in some way. Not until the *big bang* breakup in my relationship with my pastor friend did I come to realize just about everyone has unintentionally derived mental issues. I discovered almost everyone I spoke with was on some kind of depression or anti-anxiety medication. While statistics say it may only be 10-20 percent of the US population, the sampling I found around me was more like 80-90 percent.

Yes, I was happily married. But I had also bought into the belief that girls need a best buddy to pair up with and share all the details of their lives. Somewhere, I had gotten that message and imagined that "If I only had a best buddy, life would be perfect." I don't know if I actually believed life would be perfect, but a best buddy was what I thought was missing from my life. Yes, I had a wonderful family, but what I needed was...you fill in the blank. It could be anything—a car, a new job, freedom from a job, a relationship, a dog, money in the bank, a vacation, you name it. I could probably write a whole book on this thing we do to ourselves, idolizing material items, relationships, and status in the world, all because we get caught up in flesh-mind-generated ideas, instead of living from our being.

These things happen without our always being aware of them. And because we don't understand why people say, do, or don't do something, our mind makes something up just so that it can say, "I know why...." Our minds do not seem to be okay with *not* knowing something. However, our being is perfectly fine with ambiguity.

As I walked in my neighborhood with my husband the other day, he asked me about three statements I had made earlier. With each statement, he had completely misunderstood me. He had attributed totally different meanings to my words than what I'd meant. He was rather astonished to find how those simple phrases could be easily misrepresented.

Twelve years ago, around the time I began to question what was true, I was introduced to a pastor who taught weekly Bible studies. She taught *there is no wrath of God*. I asked my friend, Pam, who brought me there, to help me understand how that could be possible since the Bible clearly mentions the wrath of God. She didn't understand, either, but she felt there might be an explanation yet uncovered. Most of what this pastor taught began to make sense to me, but after several years of attending her Bible studies, I still had difficulty working certain passages out on my own and explaining some of the more challenging Scriptures to people who hadn't been taught the same things I had.

In fact, I realized this past week, while visiting my father, that we might never see eye-to-eye, having learned different things. He had learned, as a scientist, that we had evolved from Neanderthals. I had recently heard a lecture saying there is now proof that the DNA of Neanderthals is different than what it is for modern-day man, and there was an intentional modification made to our DNA since it could not have happened randomly. If I were to mention this possible fact to my father, it could suggest I felt my learning was more up-to-date and correct than his. But what if my learning were based on some inaccurate information? Then his learning would be more accurate and mine faulty. These kinds of truths are based in knowledge found by mentally learning things. Now that my father is ninety, he expresses great anguish over forgetting much of the knowledge he has acquired over his lifetime. I'm not that old, but I have also forgotten many things I've learned and experienced.

It's true our memories can be taken from us. But how about what can never be taken from us? We can lose our memories, our mental faculties, our physical strength, our health, our wealth, our status, and many other things. Could our salvation and right-standing with God depend on having any of these things, if these things can be lost? If we get dementia or suffer brain damage, must we still remember our Bible verses or that Jesus is God's son? And what about young people who haven't yet learned these truths? These are questions no person may be able to answer, so we must trust that God's ways are faithful, good, and beyond explanation of the human intellect. But what if the ways of God do not depend upon mental faculties, or having learned all the correct versus incorrect theological concepts and ideas?

The comprehension of much of Scripture seems to require knowing and understanding the language and symbolism found in the Bible, and even having knowledge of the customs of the time when the Bible was written. However, the gospel's simplicity is easily seen and understood if we search for it throughout the Scriptures. The underlying message is simple and accessible to all, regardless of physical or mental capabilities. It has to be, or God would be discriminating against people born into the *wrong* religion or life situation. Let's revisit some of the more challenging passages of Scripture and together see if we can find a truth that is not dependent upon intellect or scholarly learning, but can be directly experienced and known by all. We will first look at what happens to Satan and hell.

⁹ But fire came down from heaven and devoured them. ¹⁰ And the devil, who deceived them, was thrown into the lake of burning sulfur, where the beast and the false prophet had been thrown. They will be tormented day and night for ever and ever. (Revelation 20:9-10 NIV)

Please note that the fire came down from *heaven* and devoured the entities that had deceived God's people.

¹⁴ Then death and Hades were thrown into the lake of fire. The lake of fire is the second death. ¹⁵ Anyone whose name was not found written in the book of life was thrown into the lake of fire. (Revelation 20:14-15 NIV)

The King James version of the Bible says that death and hell were thrown into the lake of fire. Although the beast and the false prophet are tormented day and night in this lake of fire, that's because the beast and false prophet represent the created world and what is temporal and *false*. These are temporal things that have a seeming life of their own but cannot have life apart from God's Spirit. When Christ is revealed within our heart-center, and we live from God's power, we have found what is True and lasting, and there is no longer a need for our True self in Christ to be tested and proved True. At that point, and forever-more, we experience Truth, and what is constant within us, rather than conceptualizing and idolizing what is true in our minds.

God is the purifying lake of fire. He is the one who washes off all the dirt and impurities our minds attempt to label ourselves with. The fire of God (His Holy Spirit) destroys what is untrue, and It reveals what *is* True and lasting. The book of Revelation is symbolic of what happens within each person as we live under the dominion of our temporal flesh-minds and then come to directly experience our lasting Spirit-nature in Christ, which is revealed within ourselves. This revelation of Christ has been previously unknown to us, and revealed in a surprising and dramatic way. Outwardly, we will see all the shapes and outcomes of this shift in the world, but inwardly, and from our heart-center (Christ), is where it is all initiated.

For our "God is a consuming fire" (Hebrews 10:29/Deuteronomy 4:24 NIV). In a real fire, the ashes of the physical matter are left on the earth, while what is airborne rises into the heavens. It's all an analogy, for God is not a fire that can be seen with our human eyes. In attempting to understand the *second death*, let's look at 1 Corinthians 15:20-28, where it is spoken of using different words.

20 But Christ has indeed been raised from the dead, the firstfruits of those who have fallen asleep. 21 For since death came through a man, the resurrection of the dead comes also through a man. 22 For as in Adam all die, so in Christ all will be made alive. 23 But each in turn: Christ, the firstfruits; then, when he comes, those who belong to him. 24 Then the end will come, when he hands over the kingdom to God the Father after he has destroyed all dominion, authority and power. 25 For he must reign until he has put all his enemies under his feet. 26 The last enemy to be destroyed is death. 27 For he "has put everything under his feet." Now when it says that "everything" has been put under him, it is clear that this does not include God himself, who put everything under Christ. 28 When he has done this, then the Son himself will be made subject to him who put everything under him, so that God may be all in all. (NIV)

This passage explains how God becomes all in all experientially. Anything imagined (and essentially unreal) apart from God is thrown into His purifying fire. Spiritual death—and the hell caused by living in Spiritual death, plus all identities apart from Christ that are only temporal and have no actual life apart from Christ—are finally dissolved back into God. These identities never had any substance or True and lasting reality.

God is not cruel and inhumane. His plan is to help us find what is True and constant within ourselves by taking us away from what is True and constant. *Satan or the devil, who was a murderer from the beginning, and the father of lies (John 8:44)* murders or kills our ever-present Spiritual nature. But because Spirit is eternal and ever-present, it can't truly be killed or eliminated. Our True-Self is always here. It is only veiled by our flesh-minds, and temporarily hidden from our awareness. Our desire to find stability and know Him within us, as the only source of our well-being, is what enables us to consciously know and experience this Christ rock of stability and assurance.

The first death came through the man, Adam, which means *of the earth.* It is a Spiritual death...the death of Christ within...when and while we believe our True and sole nature is flesh. During this period of Spiritual death, our identity is formed by the ideas we believe about who we are conceptually, as people. This *first death* is not real from God's perspective, for *to Him, all are alive* (Luke 20:38). But from the perspective of the mind-dominated person-self, we imagine ourselves to be what is false from the perspective of Christ.

The second death also comes through a man, Christ, the Lord. It is the death of our false-self and identity based in temporal ideas, flesh bodies, and everything we do or don't do in these bodies.

Adam and Eve did not die physically after Eve was tempted by Satan in the garden. And from the perspective of God, all are alive. Adam is symbolic of our temporal flesh nature. *The first man is of the earth, earthy: the second man is the Lord from heaven (1 Corinthians 15:47 KJV). As in Adam all die (1 Corinthians 15:22 NIV).* In our flesh, and temporal nature and identity, we *all* die. There is no part of the created world that doesn't have a birth and then an eventual death. All mental and physical forms must have a death.

The second man is representative of our Spiritual nature. *So in Christ, all will be made alive (1 Corinthians 15:22 NIV). The Spirit gives life (John 6:63).* Of great importance is the statement that *all* will be made alive, rather than just some or most. The Spirit within the flesh is what enables and sustains life. Even our imagined identities are given life by Spirit, but yet as our temporal flesh identities, we think it is our flesh that has power and life somehow on its own.

I've been taught that people don't have the Holy Spirit until they ask for it, but the breath of life has been given to all flesh; otherwise, flesh would not have life or existence. It is our being, which is here at all times, that we sometimes lose sight of as we get caught up in mental activity. *The last enemy to be destroyed is (Spiritual) death (1 Corinthians 15:26 NIV).* I know it seems so dramatic and scary in the book of Revelation the way it's written symbolically. But what is being shown is how Spiritual death (and the hell caused by living in this state of ignorance of our True and constant Spiritual beingness) is eliminated by the washing away of impurities that are not *us* in the water of God's Holy and eternal Spirit, which is alive and present within us all. This is the Lake of Fire and its on-going cleansing nature.

Let's now investigate the Sheep and the Goats passage found in Matthew 25:31-46.

31 "When the Son of Man comes in his glory, and all the angels with him, he will sit on his glorious throne. 32 All the nations will be gathered before him, and he will separate the people one from another as a shepherd separates the sheep from the goats. 33 He will put the sheep on his right and the goats on his left.

34 "Then the King will say to those on his right, 'Come, you who are blessed by my Father; take your inheritance, the kingdom prepared for you since the creation of the world. 35 For I was hungry and you gave me something to eat, I was thirsty and you gave me something to drink, I was a stranger and you invited me in, ³⁶ I needed clothes and you clothed me, I was sick and you looked after me, I was in prison and you came to visit me.'

³⁷ "Then the righteous will answer him, 'Lord, when did we see you hungry and feed you, or thirsty and give you something to drink? ³⁸ When did we see you a stranger and invite you in, or needing clothes and clothe you? ³⁹ When did we see you sick or in prison and go to visit you?'

⁴⁰ "The King will reply, 'Truly I tell you, whatever you did for one of the least of these brothers and sisters of mine, you did for me.'

⁴¹ "Then he will say to those on his left, 'Depart from me, you who are cursed, into the eternal fire prepared for the devil and his angels. ⁴² For I was hungry and you gave me nothing to eat, I was thirsty and you gave me nothing to drink, ⁴³ I was a stranger and you did not invite me in, I needed clothes and you did not clothe me, I was sick and in prison and you did not look after me.'

⁴⁴ "They also will answer, 'Lord, when did we see you hungry or thirsty or a stranger or needing clothes or sick or in prison, and did not help you?'

⁴⁵ "He will reply, 'Truly I tell you, whatever you did not do for one of the least of these, you did not do for me.'

⁴⁶ "Then they will go away to eternal punishment, but the righteous to eternal life."

First of all, when the Son of Man comes in His glory (in verse 31), this is when Christ unveils Himself within our flesh. His essence and ever-present Being is exalted above our own temporal flesh identity. Our wholeness and salvation are made complete by His Spirit revealed in us. *Jesus Christ is the same yesterday and today and forever. (Hebrews 13:8 NIV).* He *has been* in us, He *is* in us, and He *will continue* to be in us. **Forever includes all the days before now, as well as now.**

The righteous sheep on the right and "you who are blessed by my father," in verse 34, are those who receive their constancy (faith) from the center of their being. We have loved and welcomed others, without even being aware we were doing anything. We visited Christ within us and fed Him, simply by abiding in our being. This visitation and abiding with Christ shows itself outwardly as we support and uplift all living things as though they are our own self. Abiding in our being, where there is no judgment and separation, we are also enabled, as people, to love without condition. From here, there is no personal gain to be attained because we are not operating from our person-self, but our Spirit-being.

The King said, *"Whatever you have done for one of the least of these brothers and sisters of mine, you have done for me." (Matthew 25:40 NIV).* This can only be True if the King, Jesus Christ, is also within even the least of our fellow men. For whatever we do to benefit anyone, we do for Christ, and also for ourselves, simultaneously. Because we are all a part of the same Spiritual Christ body, regardless of nationality, belief, thoughts, or outward behavior, anything done to Christ affects *all* within Christ.

The goats on the King's left did not feed and clothe the ever-present Spirit-Being, but served the personal-self. As a result, many personal identities are formed. There is the *me* that never seems to get it right. There is the *me* that doesn't know what to say. There is the *me* that is afraid of rejection and doesn't reach out toward others. All of these identities are formed in our flesh-minds, but they are not Truly us. They are only temporarily who we think we are. They have beginnings and ends. These personalities within us go through much tribulation, attempting to gain power and personal gain to feel secure.

It is debatable whether there can actually be eternal punishment. It may be possible the word eternal has been used here to mean something other than the same meaning used for eternal life. Typically, eternal means without beginning or end. Eternal life is the ever-present life that God is. He has no birth or death. He just is. He is constant and unchanging, and unaffected by anything created. On the other hand, punishment is something that must have a beginning and usually has an end. The reason for punishment is largely for the purpose of correcting behavior, penalizing a bad behavior to attempt to make amends, or as payment for a committed wrong. In these situations, punishment has both a beginning and an end.

Because *God has bound everyone over to disobedience so that he may have mercy on them all (Romans 11:32 NIV)*, it would appear God has plans to have mercy on all, rather than just certain people who have the correct beliefs and behavior because of the things they have done and accomplished. Furthermore, God, Himself, gave those who are disobedient a spirit of stupor.

God gave them a spirit of stupor, eyes that could not see, and ears that could not hear, to this very day (Romans 11:8, Deuteronomy 29:4, Isaiah 29:10 NIV).

I know it somewhat defies logic, but all of us know from reading stories and watching movies that if there is to be any character development or drama, there must also be challenges and/or antagonists. [28] *As far as the gospel is concerned, they are enemies for your sake... [30] Just as you who were at one time disobedient to God have now received mercy as a result of their disobedience, [31] so they too have now become disobedient in order that they too may now receive mercy as a result of God's mercy to you (Romans 11:28, 30-31 NIV).*

The challenging people we encounter in our daily lives are for *our* sake, that we be stabilized in Christ's presence within our heart-center and understand it all as a part of God's glorious plan to eventually awaken all out of their slumber. We all have a God-given role to play, and even those living the role of *antagonist* are essential to helping us find and glorify Christ within. To assume certain people are destined to be tortured without end is to misunderstand the gospel message, as well as the goodness, faithfulness, and unending mercy of God.

The goats on the King's left are asked to depart from the King and enter into the eternal fire prepared for the devil and his angels. The only thing that is eternal, without beginning or end, is God's Spirit, so the eternal fire is God's eternal fire of purification. Anything that only had temporal reality is witnessed and seen for what it is...somewhat like a dream, and only here to play a part, not having any substance or reality apart from Christ. These identities are dissolved by God's Spirit as their unreality is exposed.

While I was walking this morning with my husband, he exclaimed, "What?" as he proceeded to turn over a stick on the sidewalk. "Is it a stick? It looked just like a nail at first!" he said incredulously. I agreed. It *was* a stick that looked just like a nail until we investigated further.

As we were driving on the highway a few days ago, looking ahead in the duskiness of the early morning, I called out to my husband in concern. "Look out! There is something ahead on the road." He couldn't see it, so I explained where it was. But it turned out only to be a car traveling without headlights ahead of us. To me, it had looked like a pile of rubbish in the road because all the other cars had headlights on, and it was still slightly dark.

In both examples, an item appeared one way until we saw it with greater clarity. No longer was the stick a nail, and no longer was the car a pile of rubbish in the road. As their true identities were revealed, their false identities were annihilated. You could even say the false identities were dissolved into the Truth of God's lake of fire. **Anything that only appears to be true for a while is not ultimately True, and is, therefore, destroyed by the simple process of discovering what *is* True and constant. Its illusion no longer has any reality for us.**

The only part of us that is True, reliable, and constant is the Spirit of Christ living within us. Anything else, and any other identities we temporarily assume or believe in, were never meant to be lasting, and they are destroyed at the time of Christ's revealing Himself within our being. All these other identities continue to have life for as long as we believe in them. The eternal punishment is more like the never-ending purification and refining that takes place within our being. Our True nature in Christ suffers while imposter identities take the throne. These ideas we have about ourselves, and others, were never True and could never be True because they are just ideas that come and go like the wind. **We, as people and Spirit, suffer while we believe and buy into our mind-generated flesh identities. But our suffering is what motivates us to find Truth and our way out of the suffering. This suffering is the actual fire and wrath of God. It is a tool of God to help us find Him within our being, rather than trusting in all the temporal trappings in their various forms within the world.**

When King Jesus separates the sheep from the goats, He says that whether or not you have fed, clothed, and taken care of the sick or imprisoned, you have also done the same to Him. He lives within *all*. Could King Jesus then, in the same story, sentence certain people/goats to a never-ending existence in hell, if He would also be doing it to Himself? For everything that we or He does to even the least one has been done to Jesus, Himself. Think about it! Think long and hard, and know Jesus could not have meant the goats are tortured without an end to the torture, when He has just attempted to explain to His listeners the importance of nurturing and caring for others, as though they *are* Him. He could not, in the same story, then discard the goats in the same way the goats had not looked after Him. King Jesus would be repaying evil with evil. He would be doing what much of the world does in the insecurity of their person-selves.

In times past, and perhaps even today, those in a lower social class have been looked down upon and snubbed by those in an upper social class. The lower social class or certain people-groups within particular cultures have been treated poorly and made into slaves, with limited rights. But Jesus doesn't need us to be made lesser to feel better about Himself. No, absolutely not! King Jesus cannot be subjecting any unfortunate souls to a never-ending future of hell and torment. As stated earlier, the revelation of Truth and what is constantly True simultaneously eliminates what is only temporarily true and is, therefore, false. This is what transpires as Christ's Spirit-nature within our heart-center is revealed. He is made True, and all other identities apart from Him are made false and annihilated.

Let's now look at the man of lawlessness in 2 Thessalonians 2:1-14 NIV.

¹ Concerning the coming of our Lord Jesus Christ and our being gathered to him, we ask you, brothers and sisters, ² not to become easily unsettled or alarmed by the teaching allegedly from us—whether by a prophecy or by word of mouth or by letter—asserting that the day of the Lord has already come. ³ Don't let anyone deceive you in any way, for that day will not come until the rebellion occurs and the man of lawlessness is revealed, the man doomed to destruction. ⁴ He will oppose and will exalt himself over everything that is called God or is worshiped, so that he sets himself up in God's temple, proclaiming himself to be God.

⁵ Don't you remember that when I was with you I used to tell you these things? ⁶ And now you know what is holding him back, so that he may be revealed at the proper time. ⁷ For the secret power of lawlessness is already at work; but the one who now holds it back will continue to do so till he is taken out of the way. ⁸ And then the lawless one will be revealed, whom the Lord Jesus will overthrow with the breath of his mouth and destroy by the splendor of his coming. ⁹ The coming of the lawless one will be in accordance with how Satan works. He will use all sorts of displays of power through signs and wonders that serve the lie, ¹⁰ and all the ways that wickedness deceives those who are perishing. They perish because they refused to love the truth and so be saved. ¹¹ For this reason God sends them a powerful delusion so that they will believe the lie ¹² and so that all will be condemned who have not believed the truth but have delighted in wickedness.

¹³ But we ought always to thank God for you, brothers and sisters loved by the Lord, because God chose you as firstfruits to be saved through the sanctifying work of the Spirit and through belief in the truth. ¹⁴ He called you to this through our gospel, that you might share in the glory of our Lord Jesus Christ.

In reading through this passage about the man of lawlessness, it sounds fascinatingly like the sheep and the goats. For *God has bound everyone over to disobedience so that he may have mercy on them all (Romans 11:32 NIV)*. Not one person has escaped being bound or enslaved to disobedience, and not one person will escape the "man of lawlessness" having power over them. God has done this intentionally as a part of His plan to help us find and know Truth experientially.

Before being gathered together with and in Christ, as His glorious Spiritual body, we must first face the tribulation of living as the first man, *Adam*, who was of the earth, earthy. Back in Chapter 2, we discussed how Adam is symbolic of our temporal flesh-nature. Adam may have been a real man, but the events of his life also show us a picture of how man first came to believe he was separated from God.

The first man, Adam, was given the breath of God, or Holy Spirit, to give him individual life, but he ended up falling asleep to his True Spiritual nature. Instead, he clothed himself with the fig leaves of religion, believing his True and unadulterated self was incomplete and lacking in some way. He became deceived by the idea of a separation between himself and his Spiritual-self, or Christ within. It was by the sweat of his brow and hard labor that he attempted to work his way back to God. Religion happens when we have ideas about how we are separated from God and, therefore, need to do certain things to find salvation or wholeness.

Some people, in their mind-made separation, become addicted to drugs to find a measure of peace. Some people buy material items in an attempt to be surrounded by abundance. Some people find their way into positions of power hoping to feel great, powerful, and above others. Some people look for sex or relationships as a solution to the feelings of separateness. We all must do these external things, and go through the inevitable disappointments, before we lose our faith in them. Some people even do many good things to benefit themselves and others, hoping to find a sense of accomplishment and closeness with God. It is not usually until we have suffered enough that we stop looking for an external savior to solve our feelings of separation and lack.

While we are looking for something or someone in the world to fix us, we are also blaming people and situations in the world for our difficulties. Our focus and attention is on physical things in the world. We assume these things are either the cause of our suffering, or what will hopefully alleviate our suffering. I know this because I have lived this reality. You know this also if you have lived through challenging times. Sometimes, we even blame God for our troubles, but that only happens when we think of ourselves as a temporal flesh body, and Him as someone Spiritual and separate from us. While we are living with a strong belief in our reality as a flesh-person, or conceptualizing ourselves as a Spiritual being, we are living under the spirit of the Antichrist, or man of lawlessness. We really can't help it. God is not accusing us or sentencing us to never-ending torment. He is the One who sends us the powerful delusion to believe the lie. *They perish because they refused to love the truth and so be saved. 11 For this reason God sends them a powerful delusion so that they will believe the lie 12 and so that all will be condemned who have not believed the truth but have delighted in wickedness (1 Thessalonians 2:10-12 NIV).*

God sends the powerful delusion to believe the lie. It is intentional that we must do this. The Amplified Classic version says all will be judged or condemned who have not believed the truth. *...people are destined to die once, and after that to face judgment (Hebrews 9:27 NIV).* This is not a new message. It is the same one again. People are destined to die once Spiritually, and after that, to face judgment and feelings of separation. This is us *living as the first man of the earth...* fleshly and with a dominant flesh identity. This is the *man doomed to destruction.* The flesh is temporal and does not have ever-present or ever-lasting life. The *man doomed to destruction* is the dominant flesh identity and all the other imaginings that set themselves up in the temple of God and proclaim themselves to be God. *¹⁶ Don't you know that you yourselves are God's temple and that God's Spirit dwells in your midst? ¹⁷ If anyone destroys God's temple, God will destroy that person; for God's temple is sacred, and you together are that temple (1 Corinthians 3:16-17 NIV).* If *anyone* destroys that temple, God will destroy that person. The person destroyed is the flesh personality exalting itself and taking credit for who you are, as Spirit. It is also known as the *voice in the head* pretending to be who we are. But it cannot be who we are if we hear and witness this voice. We are the unseen Spirit witness of all the voices and appearances of people and things that come and go. Once again, *we* are the temple of God, and God's Spirit dwells in the midst of our being. Any other identity we buy into, or believe to be us, will be destroyed by the Truth of God's Spirit revealing Himself within the midst of our being.

He (Christ) has appeared once for all at the culmination of the ages to do away with sin by the sacrifice of himself. ²⁷ Just as people are destined to die once, and after that to face judgment, ²⁸ so Christ was sacrificed once to take away the sins of many; and he will appear a second time, not to bear sin, but to bring salvation to those who are waiting for him. (Hebrews 9:26-28 NIV)

Not only was Christ sacrificed in the person of Jesus Christ living on the earth two thousand years ago, to bear and endure the results of the sin and separation of the world at the time, but He has also been sacrificed within our very flesh while we are ignorant of His Presence and Spirit-nature within us. He must bear our personal sin and illusion of separation until He comes a second time in the Day of the Lord and our gathering together in Him. When and as we continually experience our Spirit-nature, this is the Day of the Lord.

Though Christ could come again as a singular man in the flesh, since He came before in this way, His coming again in the same manner would continue to perpetuate a perceived separation between one

Holy Man in the flesh and everyone else in the flesh. Flesh personalities are individualized and based in separation. Only the Spirit is One and already joined in oneness.

The Absolute Truth in Christ, must be found within our very midst so that it becomes a proven reality that we live from daily, rather than a conceptualized ideology we need to work toward finding and then somehow living out.

There is nothing you must do to earn a feeling of completeness. You already have it within the center of your being. As you read my words, put your attention on the center of your being and focus on slowing your breath. If you have any irritations or confusion in your mind, allow them to still be there and simply bring your attention away from these thoughts and into the calmness of your being. You can sort out all those troubling thoughts later. Right now, allow the emptiness and spaciousness found in your being to expand and be dominant. Stay here for as long as you like. You need not leave this calm place. Focus on this peace and stability wherever you go.

As we move on to look at some other potential mind-blocks to freedom, I leave you with this great Truth, which must pervade every Scripture passage you read from here on. God is not bipolar—one way today and another way tomorrow. It is only our changing place of perception that colors and shapes our understanding of Him and the world around us. God's plan has always been to bring us all to a direct and experiential knowing of Him. Some do not believe this because of the trials they are going through in imagined separation from His Spirit. It's all okay because it is our imagined separation that eventually brings us back to the Truth. We continue to need the world of tribulation and the man of lawlessness, who is doomed to destruction, to create trouble for us so we might also find what is True and constant in our very being, and not far away, as we have imagined.

9 For God did not appoint us to suffer wrath but to receive salvation through our Lord Jesus Christ. 10 He died for us so that, whether we are awake or asleep, we may live together with him. (1 Thessalonians 5:9-10)

When we are awake, we are aware of Christ's Presence and living within it, as our True and experienced identity. When we are asleep, we are unaware of Christ's presence within, and living from a belief in our mind-made identities, thinking the voice in the head is us, and experiencing ourselves only as a temporal flesh-person. To God, and from God's perspective, *all are alive (Luke 20:38)*. There is no True death, only a temporary Spiritual death, which is analogous to being asleep. Some people are awake, experiencing Spirit beingness, and some are asleep, and not yet experiencing this Reality. Christ died for us so that it matters not whether we are awake or asleep, for we are still living together with Him, either way. We can never be separated from Him except in our minds and beliefs. The Truth we will come to know experientially, rather than as an abstract idea. God will make it come to pass because it is all part of His great plan for all humankind. We can relax because it is not our person-selves that need to make it come about. It is Christ who will reveal Himself to us, and within us, at the appointed time.

14

The Rich Man and Lazarus, Narrow Gate, and Blasphemy of the Holy Spirit

I wanted to go so much! My friend, Pam, was going to a Christian conference in Charleston, South Carolina, with her church and had invited me to ride along in the van they were renting. Although the admission was about $100, I could save money by staying with my sister instead of at the hotel with the rest of the group. The only problem was we didn't have the $100. I prayed and still felt I should go. I asked God to miraculously provide the money so I could go. I had great faith that the money could and would appear. Even after the time of departure came and went, I still held out hope that extra money would come in so I could drive myself there. But the reality that I was not going quickly became apparent. I cried. I became depressed. I had a strong faith that God would provide where there didn't seem to be a way, but my faith in being able to go hadn't appeared to do any good. Not only was I missing out on an eye-opening conference, but also on fellowship with my current friends and the opportunity to make new friendships. I was quite devastated. God had let me down, and I began to despair of my seemingly endless financial difficulties and lack of friends to socialize with.

It took many days to recover from my disappointment. It wasn't until after my friend returned and told me the atmosphere in the van had been tense and stifling that I began to feel better. Perhaps it had been for the best that I hadn't gone. My friend told me the conference had been great, but I wouldn't have wanted to be on the four-hour van ride each way. Soon after, my husband suggested I investigate whether recordings were made of the conference. I wasn't very hopeful since there is typically a substantial charge for such things. But to my amazement, after making a phone call, I discovered I could get CDs of the entire conference for free! What? Yes, please! Suddenly, what had at first seemed to be one more unfortunate event in my already long list, was, in reality, a revealed blessing in disguise. If I had gone to the conference, I may not have even realized CDs would be made available a couple of weeks later. And with those free CDs, I was able to listen repeatedly until the messages sank in. I was also able to share the messages with other friends. Time and time again, I have discovered what, at first glance, appears to be the worst thing in the world later is revealed as one of the best things that could have happened. Of course, I don't know any of this while going through my disappointments. It is only in hindsight that such blessings are revealed.

I have found it can be the same way with many Scripture passages. At first, they appear one way, but looking at them from another perspective, their whole meaning and hidden blessing is revealed. Please look at every Scripture passage with new eyes, as though you haven't been taught anything at all before. Let your mind be open to possibilities that reveal the goodness of God in every circumstance. I have closed off my mind too many times. Don't make the same mistakes I've made.

⁶ Your boasting is not good. Don't you know that a little yeast leavens the whole batch of dough? ⁷ Get rid of the old yeast, so that you may be a new unleavened batch—as you really are. For Christ, our Passover lamb, has been sacrificed. ⁸ Therefore let us keep the Festival, not with the old bread leavened with malice and wickedness, but with the unleavened bread of sincerity and truth. (1 Corinthians 5:6-8 NIV)

The *unleavened bread of sincerity and truth* is us, as we *really* are. This sincere *us* is not the us that we or others believe us to be. The sincere and True *us* is without any mind-generated form or identity. To hear the wisdom of the Holy Spirit, we must rest in the I AMness of Christ, in our heart-center. In this place, there is no prior teaching (or leaven) to infiltrate our whole line of thinking and reasoning. Here, in the pureness of being, we can experientially know Truth and hear God's teachings above the wisdom and teachings of men using human reasoning and philosophies.

Let us first rediscover the teachings found in "The Rich Man and Lazarus." To find the context and teachings Jesus is hoping to impart by sharing this parable, let's also look at some of the verses just prior to the story in the Amplified Classic version of Luke 16.

12 And if you have not proved faithful in that which belongs to another [whether God or man], who will give you that which is your own [that is, the true riches]?

If we consider the *"true riches"* that are our own, as the ever-present Christ essence of our being, and what can never be taken from us, we know the inestimable worth compared to the temporal riches of the world, which are only here for a time. But if we don't even value what is rare and temporal and given to us on loan, how could we appreciate what is always here and our very own forever?

13 No servant is able to serve two masters; for either he will hate the one and love the other, or he will stand by and be devoted to the one and despise the other. You cannot serve God and mammon (riches, or anything in which you trust and on which you rely).

Jesus explains that it is not possible to serve two masters simultaneously. We cannot serve our Adam, flesh-nature, and also our Christ, Spirit-nature, at the same time.

14 Now the Pharisees, who were covetous and lovers of money, heard all these things [taken together], and they began to sneer at and ridicule and scoff at Him.

[15] But He said to them, You are the ones who declare yourselves just and upright before men, but God knows your hearts. For what is exalted and highly thought of among men is detestable and abhorrent (an abomination) in the sight of God.

The Pharisees declared themselves righteous on account of the Law of Moses they were able to keep. God knew their hearts because it is where God lived within them. God also knew their heart-centers were not being exalted. The Pharisees were living under the dominion of their temporal flesh-minds, which created their identities based in what they could accomplish as people.

[16] Until John came, there were the Law and the Prophets; since then the good news (the Gospel) of the kingdom of God is being preached, and everyone strives violently to go in [would force his own way rather than God's way into it].

Even though John the Baptist had brought the message of the good news that the kingdom of God was here and within reach of everyone, the Law still had its hold on people, and especially the Pharisees. John had told the people to repent and turn away from the old ways of seeing a mental separation and sin between themselves and God. Letting go of these mental concepts would enable them to find the stability and faith in the center of their hearts. However, they were still trying to get into the kingdom of God by works and diligently studying the Scriptures to determine how.

[17] Yet it is easier for heaven and earth to pass away than for one dot of the Law to fail and become void.

The Law is more than commands we must follow to be like Christ. The Law is what our heart-centers are obedient to without striving. The Law cannot fail and become void because it is the inherent nature of Christ, who is ever-present within us all. Heaven and earth are parts of the creation and, therefore, can and will pass away at some point.

However, the Law is the revealed nature of Christ, which never passes away.

18 Whoever divorces (dismisses and repudiates) his wife and marries another commits adultery, and he who marries a woman who is divorced from her husband commits adultery. (Luke 16:12-18 AMPC)

At first glance, this little tidbit of information almost seems out of context, and it is a bit odd that Jesus would recite the Law to the Pharisees, who were already masters at finding ways of outwardly following the Law. However, I believe Jesus was coming at these statements more from a Spiritual context than a *life in the body* sort of meaning. Or to be more exact, He was using the example of adultery in the body to explain Spiritual adultery. If we, as Spirit, divorce who we are married to or are continually joined together with (Christ), and become joined or identified with any other, we are creating Spiritual adultery. We become divided or divorced from our True identity in Christ.

Let's now read the story of "The Rich Man and Lazarus" in Luke 16:19-31 NIV.

19 "There was a rich man who was dressed in purple and fine linen and lived in luxury every day. 20 At his gate was laid a beggar named Lazarus, covered with sores 21 and longing to eat what fell from the rich man's table. Even the dogs came and licked his sores.

22 "The time came when the beggar died and the angels carried him to Abraham's side. The rich man also died and was buried. 23 In Hades, where he was in torment, he looked up and saw Abraham far away, with Lazarus by his side. 24 So he called to him, 'Father Abraham, have pity on me and send Lazarus to dip the tip of his finger in water and cool my tongue, because I am in agony in this fire.'

25 "But Abraham replied, 'Son, remember that in your lifetime you received your good things, while Lazarus received bad things, but now he is comforted here and you are in agony. 26 And besides all this, between us and you a great chasm has been set in place, so that those who want to go from here to you cannot, nor can anyone cross over from there to us.'

²⁷ "He answered, 'Then I beg you, father, send Lazarus to my family, ²⁸ for I have five brothers. Let him warn them, so that they will not also come to this place of torment.'

²⁹ "Abraham replied, 'They have Moses and the Prophets; let them listen to them.'

³⁰ "'No, father Abraham,' he said, 'but if someone from the dead goes to them, they will repent.'

³¹ "He said to him, 'If they do not listen to Moses and the Prophets, they will not be convinced even if someone rises from the dead.'"

Now, starting from the context and understanding found in the verses before this story of "The Rich Man and Lazarus," the *rich man* is yet another example of people living from their temporal flesh nature. Those who are enthralled by the realities and luxuries of the created world, and *rich* in terms of collecting and amassing personal accomplishment and everything temporal within the created world, cannot work their way into righteousness. Neither can they get someone else to ease the distress they feel from not experientially knowing their own True riches in Christ, within the center of their own being.

As a temporal person, we can attempt to find relief from our distresses by looking to relationships, or temporal pleasures, but we will still feel insecure, separated, and fearful. The Rich Man was in agony in the fire because that is how the fire of God works. Once again, it is not a literal fire. It is a refining and corrective fire, proving and separating what is True and ever-present from what is false and temporal. It is not until we have suffered long enough with the mind-made identity of a flesh-person living in a temporal world that we begin to look for what is stable and unchanging. Only after the temporal things of the created world fail to do what we were hoping do we begin to seek what can never be taken from us.

And for those of us attempting to become more like Christ, and following all the traditional Christian teachings, doing good works, and hoping to find God...even that search must come to an impasse. It is all a part of the refining fire's work. In the case of the Rich Man, he still did not understand he already possessed what he needed. He did not need to look to Abraham or to Lazarus. As it was explained, there is a great chasm that cannot be bridged by the works of the flesh or by human intellect. No one else can find our Spirit-nature for us. And neither can we find someone's Spirit-nature for them. This is the chasm that is set in place and cannot be crossed.

With our brains, we cannot imagine or think ourselves to God, and to a place of freedom from distress. We cannot study the Scriptures over and over to finally know enough mentally about God that we can know Him experientially. We can experience God while reading Scripture. However, head-knowledge does not substitute for direct knowing.

In this story, the Rich Man lived in and from his Adam flesh nature. Lazarus lived in and from his Spirit-nature. Jesus was not telling us a story about types of people who can never discover Truth in God and, therefore, live for all eternity separated from Him. What point do you think He could make by instilling fear in our hearts and minds?

The beggar was laid at the Rich Man's gate. We could even say this story is about us. In our flesh identity, we *are* the rich man. Lazarus, depicting Christ, and His nature, has been lain at the gate of our hearts. As the *Rich Man*, Christ's Spirit in us is scorned, wounded, and rejected, longing to be acknowledged. It was the Gentiles who were scorned in Jesus' day, and who were treated as dogs, only able to receive scraps from their master's table. This story is somewhat of an analogy where Christ's Spirit-beingness within our heart-centers is treated the same as dogs and Gentiles were treated in Jesus' day by those who were Jewish and considered God's people because of their self-proclaimed righteousness. Yes, our flesh and human mind does the same thing as the self-proclaimed righteous Jew in Jesus' day.

The Rich Man had five brothers. They were all from the same family and had the same father (or source of their existence). They all had the same upbringing. They were all believing and trusting in their temporal flesh and mind-made identities to bring them to God and a place of richness. Even if a flesh body were brought back to life and the wholeness found in God, and then sent to them, it still wouldn't be real for them. They would need to experience this wholeness themselves. If they were still seeing the way to God as something apart from what they already had, they would keep attempting to earn their way through physical and mental activities. Then God, and wholeness, from the perspective of their flesh-mind, would always be somewhere else they needed to get to. They, and we, can only meet with God in Spirit and in the Truth and constancy of our Being.

Let's now dive into the meaning behind the *"narrow gate,"* as well as the *"wise and foolish builders."*

13 "Enter through the narrow gate. For wide is the gate and broad is the road that leads to destruction, and many enter through it. 14 But small is the gate and narrow the road that leads to life, and only a few find it. (Matthew 7:13-14 NIV)

21 "Not everyone who says to me, 'Lord, Lord,' will enter the kingdom of heaven, but only the one who does the will of my Father who is in heaven. 22 Many will say to me on that day, 'Lord, Lord, did we not prophesy in your name and in your name drive out demons and in your name perform many miracles?' 23 Then I will tell them plainly, 'I never knew you. Away from me, you evildoers!'

24 "Therefore everyone who hears these words of mine and puts them into practice is like a wise man who built his house on the rock. 25 The rain came down, the streams rose, and the winds blew and beat against that house; yet it did not fall, because it had its foundation on the rock.

26 But everyone who hears these words of mine and does not put them into practice is like a foolish man who built his house on sand. 27 The rain came down, the streams rose, and the winds blew and beat against that house, and it fell with a great crash." (Matthew 7:21-27 NIV)

All of us who live near the beach, or have ever been to the beach, know with certainty what happens to a sandcastle when the tide comes in. We might have the most elaborately designed castle, but no amount of shoring it up with seashells will alter the fact that we built our castle with shifting sand, and on top of sand. Sand is easily moved from here to there. It is not a stable and solidly unmoving substance.

If we are to build our house or identity on something and expect it to last, we cannot build on anything that can change or fluctuate like sand. We must discover something within us that cannot change and has the firmness of a rock.

As I go about my day, I hear this chattering, commenting voice from time-to-time. Sometimes it is silent, and other times, I hear commentary on what I do, what others do, or about the situation in general. I know this seems obvious, but if this voice isn't constant and doesn't always say the same thing, it is not stable. In fact, sometimes it argues with itself and can't even agree with itself. If we just heard Jesus' words, we will realize this temporary, fluctuating, unstable voice is not the rock we should build our house or identity on. Will we put His words into practice? Can we notice there is an *I* who hears and witnesses this chattering voice in the head? Is this *I* always present? If not, keep looking for what is stable like the rock. If we choose to make an identity out of anything that changes from moment to moment, we are building our house on shifting sand like the foolish man.

Wide is the gate, and broad is the road that leads to destruction, and many enter through that gate (Matthew 7:13 NIV). What comes naturally to human beings is trusting in our mortality as human beings. We are used to our bodies changing over time and continual chattering in our minds. From the time we are very young, we are taught our names and conditioned to believe our bodies and everything we do, or don't do in them, is who we are. We are insecure because our identity fluctuates and changes based on the nature of our surroundings and the evaluation of our personal performance. If who we think we are is based in anything mental, do you think it is ever possible to have a constant fixed position? If it acts like sand, it really is like sand. And if it's like sand, it is the wide gate that leads to destruction.

A sandcastle is not meant to have a never-ending existence. We build them for fun, understanding that the winds and tides will wash them away in time. But imagine if we believe our sandcastle identities are real and lasting. We have a great resume of things we have done for God. We have cast out evil spirits and prophesied great words using the name *Jesus*. You may even say, "It was not me who did these things. It was Jesus." But in this situation, is there a *you*, and a *Jesus*? Do you have an identity separate from Jesus, explaining that Jesus did all these things? This *you* that has its own identity apart from Christ, unfortunately, is also like sand, and destined for destruction.

In Matthew 7:21, we are told by Jesus, *"Only the One who does the will of my Father, who is in heaven, will enter into the kingdom of heaven."* The key to understanding who this "One" is can be found in John 3:13:

No one has ascended to heaven but He who came down from heaven, that is, the Son of Man who is in heaven. (John 3:13 NKJV)

The narrow gate is finding our own Spiritual identity in Christ, through direct experience. Christ is the only One who enters through the narrow gate. Not only is He the only One who enters the gate, but He *is* the gate. *I AM the gate; whoever enters through me will be saved. They will come in and go out, and find pasture (John 10:9 NIV).* The way to enter is through Christ, in Him, and *as* Him. No other identities may enter except the *True* and ever-present Spiritual Christ identity. All other identities are not known by God because they are only temporal, like shifting sand identities.

The Son of Man, who *is* in heaven, is the only one who does the Father's will. Only what is heavenly and residing in heaven can ascend and descend from heaven. *The one who is from the earth belongs to the earth and speaks as one from the earth. The one who comes from heaven is above all (John 3:31 NIV).*

Many may attempt to enter and stand knocking outside the door (Luke 13:24-25), but they will not be allowed to enter because they are mentally created identities. This has been the imagined *me.* Instead of resting in my heart-center, *I* am in my head imagining and believing in all the offenses of myself and those of the people around me. On another day, *I* am still in my head seeing all the amazing things that *I* and others do. *I* want the world to conform to my every desire, and when it doesn't, *I* become irritable. When the world does miraculously do what *I* prefer, *I* become happy. Does this look and feel like sandy sand to you? For this reason, it is not Truly me.

I say, "I am this, and I am that. I want this and I want that." Is this the blasphemy of the Holy Spirit? What I am asking is if I am mentally separating or dividing myself from Christ, am I not mentally positioning myself against Christ? As a personality, and *person-self,* I am setting myself up in opposition to the Truth of the wholeness and indivisibility of Christ's Spiritual body, Who is connected in Oneness to all through the Holy Spirit. Any personality that attempts its own individual life in imagined separation from Christ is committing blasphemy against the Holy Spirit.

[25] Jesus knew their thoughts and said to them, "Every kingdom divided against itself will be ruined, and every city or household divided against itself will not stand. [26] If Satan drives out Satan, he is divided against himself. How then can his kingdom stand? [27] And if I drive out demons by Beelzebul, by whom do your people drive them out? So then, they will be your judges. [28] But if it is by the Spirit of God that I drive out demons, then the kingdom of God has come upon you.

[29] "Or again, how can anyone enter a strong man's house and carry off his

possessions unless he first ties up the strong man? Then he can plunder his house.

³⁰ *"Whoever is not with me is against me, and whoever does not gather with me scatters.* ³¹ *And so I tell you, every kind of sin and slander can be forgiven, but blasphemy against the Spirit will not be forgiven.* ³² *Anyone who speaks a word against the Son of Man will be forgiven, but anyone who speaks against the Holy Spirit will not be forgiven, either in this age or in the age to come. (Matthew 12:25-32 NIV)*

Although the mystery of the *unforgiveable sin* has gone on and on, what if its meaning is simpler than we've thought? *Whoever is not with me, is against me (Matthew 12:30).* It's as simple as that. Although we might mentally and verbally say, "Oh yes…I am with you, King Jesus!", if we picture ourselves as a separate entity from Jesus, we are using our human minds, and our human minds are not capable of making the two one. Our human minds are designed to compare and contrast one thing versus another. One body plus another body equals two bodies, not one. In our heart-center, One Holy Spirit includes all that is Holy Spirit. Go there now and see for yourself. Anything that you witness from here is within you. You are here. Thoughts are here. Peace is here. Nothing you witness is apart from you. If we go into our minds, however, there is me and there is you. We have separate bodies and separate thoughts. Anything witnessed from here is divided and separate. Now go back and read what Jesus had to say about how every kingdom, or person divided against itself, cannot stand and will be ruined.

All behavior can be overlooked, but the imagined person-self who receives its livelihood from a false belief in its separation from Christ cannot be overlooked. It has only a mind-made existence that is shattered and dissolved in the Truth of our own heart-center. This *false-self* parading around and imitating us must be seen within our heart-center as false. If we watch closely, we will find it is just one more thing appearing within us, and not the lasting *us*. Fearful and confused thoughts…they are not us if there is a *me* witnessing them. We can, in fact, even witness the pretend self who doesn't want these fearful and confused thoughts. No worries. Simply leave the mind and settle your attention in your heart-center again. Here, we rest in Christ in our True identity. Here, we are with Christ, and not against Him. Here, we gather with Christ, rather than scatter like our divided minds tend to do. Yes, in our hearts, and from our hearts, we are entering through the narrow gate, and we are righteous through faith in Christ Jesus.

15

Satan, the Blood, Judgment, the Day of the Lord, and the Rapture Explained

This morning, as I was eating breakfast with my husband, I noticed how quiet it was. I could hear the clock in the kitchen ticking, and every small sound appeared magnified in the stillness. Just the day before, one granddaughter would ask for one thing, and before that request had been granted, the other granddaughter would ask for something entirely different. Amid all the food requests, there had been almost continual sounds coming from one or the other of them. I believe they like to experiment with hearing all the different sounds they can make. I sat at the table today enjoying the calmness, after two days of small children running about. "It's quiet," I said, acknowledging my thoughts out loud.

"If you want, you could go down the street and listen to the construction," my husband replied.

"Do you think I'm complaining?" I asked.

"Well, yes! I know you and how you tend to think," he said.

"Well, I wasn't complaining. I was just mentioning the quiet. That's all," I replied.

Since we'd both been through two days of extra voices and more sounds than usual, I was surprised my husband didn't already know I was actually a bit relieved to have the house quieter so I could think more clearly and without interruption. I was grateful and in a state of appreciation, but my husband had missed it. Even though we've been married thirty-four years, there still seem to be many situations where we misunderstand one another. And in this particular situation, it may be that my husband heard the meaning of my words based on how he was feeling at the time. It can be like that, you know. Whenever I've eaten a huge meal at dinner, and others talk about eating more, or having dessert, even the thought of eating or serving additional food to others seems repulsive to me. "Are you *sure* you are still hungry?" I may ask. I imagine my own fullness onto others. I see their situation through my own.

I've noticed reading and interpreting Scripture can be rather similar. On the days in the past when I, as a person-self, was feeling left out and alone, it was hard to find any good news in the Bible. Even what was clearly intended as good news seemed to be a reminder that I didn't have the same gifts or good relationship with God as those wonderful men and women of God. If God had promised something, I didn't have it because I was sure I was somehow defective. In times like that, I was seeing everything through emotional pain from my personal flesh-identity, and without even realizing it, I was actively looking to find the wrong in others or myself. In ignorance, I was acting as an agent of Satan, the devil. But, of course, we do this without knowing it anytime we live from our temporal, mind-generated identity. Although I've thought of Satan in the past as a specific being of destruction, I now realize he is symbolic of the voice in our heads we think is us, until we witness this voice, and know anything we see or hear is *not* us. Satan acts as the accuser in our minds until this voice no longer holds our attention and becomes as insignificant as a passing breath. That's what these verses in Revelation 12:9-10 explain. The great dragon has been (past tense) hurled down from the high places of authority. Although this has already taken place and is True now, it may not be a reality yet from the perspective of the mind-made false identity we errantly take ourselves to be.

9 The great dragon was hurled down—that ancient serpent called the devil, or Satan, who leads the whole world astray. He was hurled to the earth, and his angels with him.

10 Then I heard a loud voice in heaven say: "Now have come the salvation and the power and the kingdom of our God, and the authority of his Messiah. For the accuser of our brothers and sisters, who accuses them before our God day and night, has been hurled down. (Revelation 12:9-10 NIV)

So, the really good news is that Satan, the one who accuses us and those around us of wrongdoing and inadequacy, has been hurled down and has no lasting power over us, or in how we are in right standing with God right now. Don't do what I've done in the past and block the message of good news found in Scripture. Open your heart, and rest in your being, where Christ is alive and well. Let's continue on in this way, looking at some other big questions not yet answered.

You may still be wondering about the *blood of Christ*, written about in the Scriptures, which is considered necessary to make atonement for our sins. To discover more about this precious *blood*, let's read through what Jesus said about His body and blood.

26 While they were eating, Jesus took bread, and when he had given thanks, he broke it and gave it to his disciples, saying, "Take and eat; this is my body."

27 Then he took a cup, and when he had given thanks, he gave it to them, saying, "Drink from it, all of you. 28 This is my blood of the covenant, which is poured out for many for the forgiveness of sins. (Matthew 26:26-28 NIV) 29 I say to you, I shall not drink again of this fruit of the vine until that day when I drink it with you new and of superior quality in My Father's kingdom. (Matthew 26:29 AMPC)

In what was the Passover feast in Jesus' last supper with His disciples, Jesus refers to the bread as symbolic of His body and the wine as symbolic of His blood. We know He didn't mean the bread or wine were literally His body and blood. And in verse 29, Jesus says He won't drink the fruit of the vine again until He drinks it with us in a new and superior way in His Father's Kingdom. The new and superior way Jesus drinks the fruit of the vine with us is through communion within the Holy Spirit, as this fruit is explained in Galatians 5:22-24.

22 But the fruit of the Spirit is love, joy, peace, forbearance, kindness, goodness, faithfulness, 23 gentleness and self-control. Against such things there is no law. 24 Those who belong to Christ Jesus have crucified the flesh with its passions and desires. (NIV)

The manifested result of being in communion and oneness with Christ is experiencing the resulting fruit of the Spirit. Jesus is also the *vine*, and we are the branches connected to Him.

5 "I am the vine; you are the branches. If you remain in me and I in you, you will bear much fruit; apart from me you can do nothing. 6 If you do not remain in me, you are like a branch that is thrown away and withers; such branches are picked up, thrown into the fire and burned. (John 15:5-6 NIV)

If we remain in our heart, in our Spirit-nature, we will bear much fruit. However, if we depart from here, and live dominated by our divided flesh-mind, we will have a separate identity based in our flesh bodies. Jesus has already explained to us: *The Spirit gives life; the flesh counts for nothing (John 6:63 NIV).*

As we read through Scripture, we may be tempted to assume a literal or flesh meaning, but everything in the material world has only temporal existence. We might use material items to analogize what is eternal and lasting, but anything temporal cannot create a lasting covenant or seal between us, as people, and God, who is Spirit. Now that we are aware of this Truth, we can read through the passage in Hebrews 9, picturing the physical body and blood of Christ as having a temporal reality, pointing to an ever-present Spiritual Truth that cannot be visualized.

¹¹ But when Christ came as high priest of the good things that are now already here, he went through the greater and more perfect tabernacle that is not made with human hands, that is to say, is not a part of this creation. ¹² He did not enter by means of the blood of goats and calves; but he entered the Most Holy Place once for all by his own blood, thus obtaining eternal redemption. ¹³ The blood of goats and bulls and the ashes of a heifer sprinkled on those who are ceremonially unclean sanctify them so that they are outwardly clean. ¹⁴ How much more, then, will the blood of Christ, who through the eternal Spirit offered himself unblemished to God, cleanse our consciences from acts that lead to death, so that we may serve the living God! (Hebrews 9:11-14 NIV)

Verse 14 specifically mentions it is through the eternal ever-present Spirit that Christ offered Himself unblemished to God. The Holy Spirit *is* the blood and inherited bloodline of Christ, who is Spirit. Christ did not have an identity as a flesh-person. *⁵⁴ Whoever eats my flesh and drinks my blood has eternal life, and I will raise them up at the last day. ⁵⁵ For my flesh is real food and my blood is real drink. ⁵⁶ Whoever eats my flesh and drinks my blood remains in me, and I in them. ⁵⁷ Just as the living Father sent me and I live because of the Father, so the one who feeds on me will live because of me. ⁵⁸ This is the bread that came down from heaven. Your ancestors ate manna and died, but whoever feeds on this bread will live forever." (John 6:54-58 NIV).* Jesus is telling us the I AM Being that gives Him Life is the same I AM Being that gives us Life. We have the same Spiritual bloodline, and we must drink of it and remain in His I AM Life within us to experience His eternal and ever-present abundant Spiritual Life.

The Lord had told Moses, *"because the life of every creature is its blood. That is why I have said to the Israelites, 'You must not eat the blood of any creature, because the life of every creature is its blood; anyone who eats it must be cut off.' (Leviticus17:14 NIV).* The Jews of Jesus' day were all confused when they heard we must eat Jesus' flesh and drink His blood. This went completely against the Levitical Law. However, Jesus was not speaking about His literal flesh and blood, but about the Holy Spirit that fed and sustained His Spiritual, as well as physical, life.

If we say the literal blood of Christ cleanses our consciences from acts that lead to death so that we may serve the living God (Hebrews 9:14), wouldn't the physically shed blood on the cross from two thousand years ago have resulted in a cleansing of the entire earth at that time and forever after?

In Hebrews 9:11, we are told that when Christ came as the high priest (the only one allowed into the Holy of Holies), He went through the more perfect tabernacle or temple, not built with human hands and not a part of the creation. His flesh and our flesh are all a part of the temporarily created world. The more perfect tabernacle is unseen. These verses are attempting to show us what happened, and is still happening today in an unseen Spiritual way, by using the analogy of physically seen things.

God never wanted sacrifices and offerings (1 Samuel 15:22, Psalm 40:6, Psalm 51:16, Hosea 6:6, Hebrews 10:8). These did not please Him. However, what God and Moses wanted us to see was the resulting death of what is *perfect and unblemished* each and every time we engage in ignorant or willful acts of disobedience. The sacrifice of unblemished bulls and goats was not somehow to make up for our misdeeds or appease an angry God. Every time we are disobedient or displaying works of the flesh, we are *putting to death* the unblemished Lamb of God within ourselves. We are not living from our heart-center, where the Holy Spirit guides and directs. We are living from our flesh-minds in our flesh identities.

[19] The acts of the flesh are obvious: sexual immorality, impurity and debauchery; [20] idolatry and witchcraft; hatred, discord, jealousy, fits of rage, selfish ambition, dissensions, factions [21] and envy; drunkenness, orgies, and the like. I warn you, as I did before, that those who live like this will not inherit the kingdom of God. (Galatians 5:19-21 NIV)

And every time we are living from our flesh identities, Christ is being sacrificed and slaughtered so that our flesh receives the glory and honor. Christ is sacrificed in order for sin to take place. Jesus did not need to die in His flesh for us to be made right with God. It was sin, and the flesh-nature of the people living at the time, that crucified Jesus in the flesh. Jesus, in the flesh, took on the sin of the world at the time. He willingly died in His flesh body from what was done to Him by those who were not living from their Spiritual heart-center. The people who put Jesus to death were so immersed in their flesh identities that they were unable to be conscious and aware of their actions through their Spiritual Christ-nature. This is why Jesus said, *"Father, forgive them, for they do not know what they are doing" (Luke 23:34).* The True and ever-present Spiritual nature within themselves was not the source of their acting and did not have dominance.

The first order or way of meeting with God through a mediator requires that we follow a set of laws that ask us to be kind and thoughtful. Instead of living directly *from* the Law (Christ) in oneness, we must attempt to follow the Law (Christ). *"A mediator, however, implies more than one party; but God is One" (Galatians 3:20 NIV). In other words, there is no mediator needed within one body. A mediator is only needed between two or more bodies.* The mediator can be a person like Moses. However, the need for a mediator is first created within the mind. From the dual perspective of the human mind, we appear separated from God and one another since the mind is designed to compare one object with another object. From this viewpoint of separation, we require a mediator and cannot be loyal to God.

Christ gives us another, better way and tells us, *"Here (is the great) I AM...(beingness)...It is I who have come to do the will of the Father" (Hebrews 10:9 NIV).* Our human flesh mind cannot do the will of God. Only Christ, in our heart-center, knows and does the will of God. After we have done all we know to do in our temporal flesh identity, and finally give up, only then do we seek what is ever-present. Christ sets aside this first way of unsuccessfully achieving righteousness through our flesh identity in order to establish the second way, which is ever-lasting, and does not gratify our egos and mind-made resumes.

⁸ First he [Christ] said, "Sacrifices and offerings, burnt offerings and sin offerings you did not desire, nor were you pleased with them"—though they were offered in accordance with the law. ⁹ Then he said, "Here I am, I have come to do your will." He sets aside the first to establish the second. ¹⁰ And by that will, we have been made holy through the sacrifice of the body of Jesus Christ once for all.

¹¹ Day after day every priest stands and performs his religious duties; again and again he offers the same sacrifices, which can never take away sins. ¹² But when this priest had offered for all time one sacrifice for sins, he sat down at the right hand of God, ¹³ and since that time he waits for his enemies to be made his footstool. ¹⁴ For by one sacrifice he has made perfect forever those who are being made holy.

¹⁵ The Holy Spirit also testifies to us about this. First he says:

¹⁶ "This is the covenant I will make with them
 after that time, says the Lord.
I will put my laws in their hearts,
 and I will write them on their minds."

¹⁷ Then he adds:

"Their sins and lawless acts
 I will remember no more."

¹⁸ And where these have been forgiven, sacrifice for sin is no longer necessary. (Hebrews 10:8-18 NIV)

In our heart-center, sins and lawless acts are remembered no more. Right now, my flesh-mind is upset by having certain desired plans that cannot take place. I, as a person-self, had hoped to spend this evening and tomorrow morning finishing writing my book. But it now turns out I need to watch my sweet young grandchildren. And on top of that, the younger one is sick with a bad cough and fever. But as soon as I close my eyes and enter my heart-center…and even before…I can see this meaningless activity of the mind. It worries about worst-case scenarios that haven't happened. However, I see it all. I even see the imagined *one* who is upset, who is only temporal and living from the mental conditioning of the past. Going deeper within my heart, all of this turmoil passes away. Come there with me, and know this place in yourself to be True and ever-present. It is not somewhere else you need to get to. It is right here and right now.

Keep in mind part of the good news that *[8] All inhabitants of the earth will worship the beast—all whose names have not been written in the Lamb's book of life, the Lamb who was slain from the creation of the world (Revelation 13:8 NIV).* Since *all* inhabitants of the earth will worship the beast, or our mind-made identity, it has been planned for and factored in. It is not only normal, but necessary, to worship this beastly false identity, and live under the burden and oppression caused by these false identities. These false identities we create in our minds are the ones whose names have not been written in the Lamb's Book of Life. Yes, the Lamb who was slain from the creation of the world, rather than two thousand years ago.

Jesus came in a flesh body and was slain as an innocent Lamb. However, the universal Lamb, or Holy Spirit living within human-kind, was slain at the same time the created world in the mind began. The names not written in the Lamb's Book of Life are the ones created by us, apart from our Christ identity. Yes, you guessed it! All those names we have called ourselves by, including the ones that give us in-dividual significance, are not written in the Lamb's Book of Life. Only our True and lasting, innocent Lamb-Self, is written in the Lamb's Book of Life. The sacrifice of the Spiritual body of Christ, and our ever-present Lamb-Self, is the one-time sacrifice for sin. Sins and law-less acts are a result of living in ignorance of our ever-present Spiritual Christ nature. Once this is seen and witnessed by Christ within our heart-center, it can be forgiven and remembered no more, just as I see cars pass by on the road, which have no lasting significance.

So, what about the great and terrible day of the Lord, the judgment, and rapture? There are so many passages that speak of this great and terrible day of the Lord.

[10] For we must all appear and be revealed as we are before the judgment seat of Christ, so that each one may receive [his pay] according to what he has done in the body, whether good or evil [considering what his purpose and motive have been, and what he has achieved, been busy with, and given himself and his attention to accomplishing]. (2 Corinthians 5:10 AMPC)

I know it sounds as though we, as people, must be continually amassing wonderful works to appear on our end-of-life resume, but with God, things tend to turn out a little differently than our human mind thinks and imagines. *[11] For who knows a person's thoughts except their own spirit within them? In the same way no one knows the thoughts of God except the Spirit of God (1 Corinthians 2:11 NIV).*

I have listened to and read about several near-death experiences, and interestingly, in most of them, there is a *life-review*. During the life-review, we are not bound by our earthly bodies and minds, and are able to go through our entire lifetime of experiences knowing the repercussions of each one of our actions, whether kind or unkind. Not only do we feel the joy and pain of others around us, but we also see and understand why we did what we did. With regards to our selfish acts, we see how they were all attempts to protect and promote a certain image of ourselves that was never real. We see our actions and the circumstances that led up to these actions, whether good or bad, and see them all without judgment. Sometimes in these experiences, a Christ-figure helps us through our life-review, providing insight or comfort when needed. While we are caught up in our self-image and temporal identities, we will have all kinds of fears and points of view that we don't realize are filtering the world around us.

One of my greatest fears, as a person-self, has been a fear of being rejected and alone. As a child, I didn't like the feeling of being ridiculed. Looking back on it, I shouldn't have taken it personally since it is just what insecure children do to attempt feeling more in control and secure. But having my peers poke fun at my name, my clothes, or my anything made me feel rejected and separated from them. I reasoned there must be something about me that was inadequate or strange in a repulsive way. As a teenager, I mostly felt like a stranger looking in at those who were much more put-together than I was. I honestly had no idea anyone else was struggling with these same issues. I thought it was just defective *me*.

I saw the world and all the events that happened to me through this lens of inadequacy and fear of being left out, and then I experienced the resulting aloneness. I had a few friends, but that wasn't enough to change my skewed perceptions. If someone had tried to explain to me then that I wasn't this self I thought I was, but the one witnessing this self, and all its troubles, it would have made no sense to me, I'm sure. I was much too wrapped up in being a person-self and trying to cope as one. I would have considered this information purely from a mental point-of-view. If someone had sat with me and taught me how to breathe more deeply and focus on my heart-center and inner well-being, I may have turned out to be entirely different. But no one did that, and it was not my path to take. Even though the Israelites who left Egypt, in Moses's day, were not so very far from the Promised Land, they took the long way there, for the purposes of removing all their habits as slaves. Yes, sometimes the fastest way is not the way that leads us to True and lasting freedom.

Going back to our *judgment* and *life-review*, all our fears and resulting behaviors are revealed for what they are. Our True and lasting nature is revealed, as well.

While here on earth, there is another principle at work. [37] *"Do not judge, and you will not be judged. Do not condemn, and you will not be condemned. Forgive, and you will be forgiven.* [38] *Give, and it will be given to you. A good measure, pressed down, shaken together and running over, will be poured into your lap. For with the measure you use, it will be measured to you." (Luke 6:37-38 NIV).*

Although it's possible this passage could be interpreted to mean we will receive some kind of reward or punishment after this lifetime, it's also just as possible Jesus is helping us to find joy and freedom here on earth in our current flesh bodies. You see, while I was judging others as better than me, they treated me as though they *were* better than me. It was as though I was holding up a mirror for people to treat me with the same lens through which I saw myself.

During the time I became extremely depressed, all I wanted was to experientially know the love of God from the people around me, but because I didn't feel love coming from myself or *for* myself, it was as though I was creating more evidence of the lack of love and appreciation for me, as a person. I'm glad I didn't know it while it took place, but I later found out my husband had considered leaving me during this time. I had believed so much that others would be better off without me that people around me were actually thinking the same thing!

The catalyst that brought me out of depression was invisible to me at the time, but a great part of my healing happened while I spent time writing. Without reading or learning about any kind of technique for *going into my heart-center*, I instinctively went there whenever waiting for words to come. During the time I felt deep emotional hurt from my friend distancing herself from me, my mind would alternate between remembering the fun we'd shared together and feeling angry and hurt. Sometimes, during this time, I would write a letter to my friend to apologize and keep the lines of communication open. Because my mind was so fickle, I would need to access the center of my being to remember all the love I held for her. Most of the time, I wouldn't want to stop writing because I felt so healed during this time. Eventually, over a year later, my friend and I made amends and experienced a better friendship than we'd ever had before.

Could these occurrences actually be like the great white throne judgment? In viewing the past through my inmost being, I could see and feel some of the issues my friend must have been dealing with at the time. All that was there, in this particular judgment and seeing, was compassion, great caring, and appreciation. Even all the troubles I had gone through were seen to have served the purpose of bringing me to this place of greater healing. I had sudden clarity about why I had written the email that caused the breakup of our friendship. Knowing what I know now, or during this time of clarity, I would not have written the email. But at the time, it seemed like the best thing to do…and actually it was…in a strange sort of way. If I hadn't written the letter, and if my friend hadn't responded the way she had, I might still be a ginormous mental mess, and I never would have sought out answers to the questions about how to find God and Truth. At this point, all I can feel is gratitude for the opportunity to move beyond where I was as a temporal person-identity. Interestingly, as I see others through my heart, there is no judgment, and likewise, I feel no judgment from them.

In John 12:46-47, Jesus explains it is not He who judges, for He has come into the world to save it. If anyone hears His message and words but does not believe or trust in them, He still doesn't judge anyone (John 12:47). He has come into our hearts as the Light that enables us to see the created world. **As temporal people, we are a part of this created world, but as a part of Christ's Spiritual body, we are what is ever-present and without end, observing the created world.** Whoever trusts in this place or Kingdom of God, within themselves, is not judged and does not judge. However, those who identify with their flesh and mind-made personality are judged because they are living within their divided flesh minds, viewing the world and themselves from this place of mind-generated judgment. When we are convicted of our True and lasting Spiritual identity in Christ, through direct experience, the old identity, based in misunderstanding of what is True and real, will fade away.

⁴⁶ I have come as a Light into the world, so that whoever believes in Me [whoever cleaves to and trusts in and relies on Me] may not continue to live in darkness.

⁴⁷ If anyone hears My teachings and fails to observe them [does not keep them, but disregards them], it is not I who judges him. For I have not come to judge and to condemn and to pass sentence and to inflict penalty on the world, but to save the world.

⁴⁸ Anyone who rejects Me and persistently sets Me at naught, refusing to accept My teachings, has his judge [however]; for the [very] message that I have spoken will itself judge and convict him at the last day. (John 12:46-48 AMPC)

Jesus' teachings that we reject are not only the words He speaks to us in Scripture, as well as the teachings given to us by wise people, but also His Presence within our heart revealing what is always constant and here with us, even now. His very Spirit Presence within us, this eternal Logos, will convict us at the last day.

Many are the Scripture passages that speak of the coming of the Lord at the end of time. As is typical with Scripture, there may be literal meanings derived from the material objects represented, but there is also a more ever-present and universal Spiritual interpretation that can be ascertained from the symbolic meanings within the Bible.

⁵ To him who loves us and has freed us from our sins by his blood, ⁶ and has made us to be a kingdom and priests to serve his God and Father—to him be glory and power for ever and ever! Amen.

⁷ "Look, he is coming with the clouds,"
  and "every eye will see him,
even those who pierced him";

  and all peoples on earth "will mourn because of him."

So shall it be! Amen.

8 "I am the Alpha and the Omega," says the Lord God, "who is, and who was, and who is to come, the Almighty." (Revelation 1:5-8 NIV)

Jesus Christ is the One who has freed us from our sins and shortcomings, by His blood (Holy Spirit), and has made *us* to be a kingdom of priests who can enter the Holy of Holies, in our Spiritual nature. Look! He is coming with the manifested glory of God (clouds). All will see and know Him, including those who, at one time, were unaware of His Presence within their hearts and the stabilizing Life-giving Essence within all creation. The Great I AM Beingness is the Beginning and the End, who *was* and who *is*, and who *is to come*. The One Essence who *has always* been with us, who *is* currently with us, and who *will always* be with us. All the temporary people-identities will mourn because of Him, for those identities are part of the created world that cannot have eternal and ever-present Life.

1 "Surely the day is coming; it will burn like a furnace. All the arrogant and every evildoer will be stubble, and the day that is coming will set them on fire," says the LORD Almighty. "Not a root or a branch will be left to them. 2 But for you who revere my name, the sun of righteousness will rise with healing in its rays. And you will go out and frolic like well-fed calves. 3 Then you will trample on the wicked; they will be ashes under the soles of your feet on the day when I act," says the LORD Almighty.

4 "Remember the law of my servant Moses, the decrees and laws I gave him at Horeb for all Israel.

5 "See, I will send the prophet Elijah to you before that great and dreadful day of the LORD comes. 6 He will turn the hearts of the parents to their children, and the hearts of the children to their parents; or else I will come and strike the land with total destruction." (Malachi 4:41-6 NIV)

But for you who revere my name (verse 2)…the name which is *above* any name which can be spoken or uttered…the name which is not a name or defined identity…but the Great I AM, Beingness within our heart-center…for you who abide here, in the shadow of the Almighty, the revealing of your inherent righteousness as Spirit within the Holy Spirit will enable you to frolic and play like well-fed calves wherever you go and whatever you do. The temporal flesh-identity and the trials in life created by it will trouble you no more.

Before the great and dreadful day of the Lord, the Spirit of Elijah, which helps us to repent and turn away from our mind-generated identity and separation, will awaken our hearts to the love of God and the mind of Christ within.

After searching, I found one passage that actually explains what it is that Jesus Christ is judging in the day of the Lord.

34 And Peter opened his mouth and said: Most certainly and thoroughly I now perceive and understand that God shows no partiality and is no respecter of persons,

35 But in every nation he who venerates and has a reverential fear for God, treating Him with worshipful obedience and living uprightly, is acceptable to Him and sure of being received and welcomed [by Him].

36 You know the contents of the message which He sent to Israel, announcing the good news (Gospel) of peace by Jesus Christ, Who is Lord of all— (Acts 10:34-36 AMPC)

42 And He charged us to preach to the people and to bear solemn testimony that He is the God-appointed and God-ordained Judge of the living and the dead.

43 To Him all the prophets testify (bear witness) that everyone who believes in Him [who adheres to, trusts in, and relies on Him, giving himself up to Him] receives forgiveness of sins through His name. (Acts 10: 42-43 AMPC)

First of all, verse 36 mentions knowing the message of the good news Gospel of peace by Jesus Christ, who is Lord of *all*. Jesus Christ is not Lord of some, but Lord of *all*. If that is indeed True, then His

Lordship must apply across the board. Anyone who doesn't acknowledge His Lordship and is not obedient must, therefore, be operating under a false identity.

In verse 43, Jesus is the God-ordained Judge of the Spiritually living and the Spiritually dead. Any identity apart from His identity is not True and ever-present. These identities are *dead* because they are only imagined within the human mind and have no real or lasting life. Christ reveals and judges between what is eternal and what is temporal. In Him, He enables us to see from His perspective.

Today, my six-year-old granddaughter, Alana, asked me about the puppies on her notebook. And I made the comment that they are, of course, not *real* puppies. They are just pictures or images of puppies. She knew that, but it reminded me of how we sometimes get confused about what truly *is* real. The puppies, themselves, were real. However, the image of them was not. When we create an image or idea in our minds of anything, it has a sort of reality, but only one that is temporary while we hold that image in our minds. As soon as we think of something else, it is gone from our minds. Even the true objects, themselves, only have a temporary reality. The person or object serves its purpose, and then it is there no more. **What lasts, however, is the ever-present Essence within. It is this ever-present Essence, in Him, which Christ has come to separate from what is false and temporal in the created world.**

Perhaps one of the longer and more complete passages of Scripture describing the chain of events leading up to the great and dreadful day of the Lord is found in Joel 2. Before the passage below, there is a description of a great and fearful army of the Lord that devours everything in its path. Once again, the only things that are actually devoured are what have only a temporal existence. Anything that is temporary must be revealed for what it is so we can find what is everlasting within us and around us. And after all the temporal identities are devoured, God pours out His Spirit upon *all* people, not just some specially chosen ones. For God is not a respecter of persons showing favoritism to a select few. The sun that is turned to darkness and the moon to blood is a picture of many possible things. Because the blood symbolizes the Life of the Spirit, the moon, which normally would be considered lifeless, embodies the fullness of Life in the Holy Spirit, within what might be considered dead…like our human bodies that have no life without the Spirit of God. The darkened sun probably symbolizes the veiling of constant and True Light from the Spirit within when we are not consciously experiencing It. Of course, It is there, only darkened.

But the good news is that everyone who calls on the name of the Lord, or visits the great I AM, which is everyone's Spiritual Christ nature within, will be saved. The great mystery revealed as *Christ in you, the hope of glory*, cannot die, no matter what! It not only is in us, but It is an inseparable part of who we are. Perhaps it is only now that we can understand how we are *already* saved because of the Holy Spirit sealing the deal and existing within us all. However, until we know this Spirit-nature experientially, it will only be an idea in our minds that we need to somehow get to or acquire. There will always be a separation in our minds between where we are and where we need to arrive. This is the big trap in trying to be obedient to God or follow His laws. There will always be a separate temporal identity attempting to be made righteous or one with God. This one is not Truly us, and knowing it mentally is no substitute for experiencing His peace in our hearts.

²⁸ *"And afterward,*
    I will pour out my Spirit on all people.
Your sons and daughters will prophesy,
    your old men will dream dreams,
    your young men will see visions.
²⁹ *Even on my servants, both men and women,*
    I will pour out my Spirit in those days.
³⁰ *I will show wonders in the heavens*

and on the earth,
blood and fire and billows of smoke.
³¹ The sun will be turned to darkness
and the moon to blood
before the coming of the great and dreadful day of the LORD.

³² And everyone who calls
on the name of the LORD will be saved;
for on Mount Zion and in Jerusalem
there will be deliverance,
as the LORD has said,
even among the survivors
whom the LORD calls. (Joel 2:28-32)

So, what about the rumors of a rapture, where the people of God are taken and then there are others left behind on a horrific planet with evil running rampant? Let's check into this passage to see if there are any hidden meanings that might be good news for everyone, without exception.

²⁰ Once, on being asked by the Pharisees when the kingdom of God would come, Jesus replied, "The coming of the kingdom of God is not something that can be observed, ²¹ nor will people say, 'Here it is,' or 'There it is,' because the kingdom of God is in your midst." (Luke 17:20-21 NIV)

The Kingdom of God is in your midst, in your inner being. It cannot be pointed to as an object because it is the essence of who you are, and the Source and cause of your being and existence.

²² Then he said to his disciples, "The time is coming when you will long to see one of the days of the Son of Man, but you will not see it. ²³ People will tell you, 'There he is!' or 'Here he is!' Do not go running off after them. ²⁴ For the Son of Man in his day will be like the lightning, which flashes and lights up the sky from one end to the other. ²⁵ But first he must suffer many things and be rejected by this generation. (Luke 17:22-25 NIV)

According to these verses, the Son of Man will not be, and is not, a person that can be followed. People will suggest Christ will come again in a specific flesh body, but if that were true, we could go running after them and attempt to follow them just like the disciples in Jesus' day. Jesus tells us people will suggest Christ will come in a specific form, but He is Spirit and will come to all of us in the same way He came within Jesus of Nazareth. The Son of Man will illuminate the spaciousness within our heart, helping us to know His limitlessness, just as the darkened sky is lit up by lightning. But before any of this takes place, Christ's Presence within must be rejected by us, just as He was rejected by the religious leaders of the day. Outwardly, we may even be ostracized, or rejected by those we care about, or those who are immersed in religious tradition. We must all go through some kind of personal tribulation and suffer in our temporal flesh identities.

26 "Just as it was in the days of Noah, so also will it be in the days of the Son of Man. 27 People were eating, drinking, marrying and being given in marriage up to the day Noah entered the ark. Then the flood came and destroyed them all. (Luke 17:26-27 NIV)

Before Christ's nature is revealed in us, we will be going about life doing the same things we have always been doing. Then the purifying waters will come and wash away everything that claims to have importance and significance but is only here today and gone tomorrow. In my case, my special friend was taken from me. This event brought on a series of hardships to whittle away at all the temporal things that capture my strong attention.

28 "It was the same in the days of Lot. People were eating and drinking, buying and selling, planting and building. 29 But the day Lot left Sodom, fire and sulfur rained down from heaven and destroyed them all.

30 "It will be just like this on the day the Son of Man is revealed. 31 On that day no one who is on the housetop, with possessions inside, should go down to get them. Likewise, no one in the field should go back for anything. 32 Remember Lot's wife! 33 Whoever tries to keep their life will lose it, and whoever loses their life will preserve it. ³⁴ I tell you, on that night two people will be in one bed; one will be taken and the other left. ³⁵ Two women will be grinding grain together; one will be taken and the other left." (Luke 17:28-35 NIV)

As we go into our heart-center (housetop and high vantage point), we shouldn't try to hold on to any ideas or thoughts (possessions of the mind). When our self-image feels threatened, we shouldn't go looking for ways to boost it. Even when we are tempted to build our confidence in all the negative things that have happened to us, or all the ways we, as a person, are a failure, we must resist the urge even to follow this train of thought or identification. Let all that go. Be empty of all this. **For whoever loses their ideas about who they are will find their stability in what is constantly themselves.**

The two people in one bed, or grinding grain, are the True and the false self. The one taken is the false self (apart from Christ), whose identity is based on a mind-made image formed from past events and beliefs. The one person who is left is the True Self (in Christ), who does not have a mind-made identity that needs continual reassurance. This person lives from the Spirit of God in the center of their being. This person witnesses events and behaviors come and go, but his identity does not take on any shape, whatsoever. *"You shall not make for yourself an image in the form of anything in heaven above or on the earth beneath or in the waters below." (Exodus 20:4 NIV).* The True Spiritual *You* does not take on images in the form of anything in heaven or on earth.

Not only is the True Self and resulting True person not an image in the mind, but this True Christ self within is continual and ever-present. It cannot be taken away any more than the Holy Spirit can be taken away. These Truths are the foundation and essence of everything created and seen in the world. Were this Essence of Holy Spirit removed from the world, there would be no visible world.

From here on out, choose to seek out the life-giving message of good news that Jesus Christ came to bring the world. If God's coming to earth in a specific, physically seen, flesh body meant the condemnation for many who don't believe in His coming in this way, how could it have been beneficial? If this were His purpose, it would have been better that He not come in the flesh at all.

No, Christ came to proclaim the kingdom of heaven in our midst, in our very inner being. He wanted us to know it was near to us, rather than far off. He wanted us to know this divine Kingdom was not something we could observe coming, because it is not an idea, person, object, or place to be witnessed. The only thing we cannot witness and point to is the essence of our being and the very place of our witnessing, which cannot be seen. This Kingdom is where we live and dwell as Spirit. Being unaware and ignorant of this Essence cannot nullify or change its existence. It is holy and set apart from the created world, not affected by darkened minds or wickedness in any form. This is the super-great news for all of humanity, and what will ultimately set the world free from believing in the powerful delusion of the mind-generated self and its ways of attempted self-preservation. Thanks be to God!

Once again, set aside all your troubles, questions, or confusion. Place your attention on your heart-center and take a deep breath. Stay here and enjoy the presence of Christ in your midst. Nothing more needs to be done for now. Rest here in peace and continue here in peace as you go about your day. Trials and agitations may come and go, but peace remains. Thank you, thank you, thank you.

16

Living in and from a Place of Freedom

Listening to my friend talk, I suddenly became aware I didn't have the usual sensation of having a body. I had been so captured by being there in my essence that having a body just wasn't on my radar. I wasn't even sure I remembered how to move, but slowly and intentionally, I discovered I really was still in my body and could move it.

Looking back on the situation later, there was a desire to reproduce that amazing sensation, but now, I realize it was just a passing phenomenon, and not something to worship, exalt, or bring back to life. Anything I truly need is here right now and can be found in the Essence of my being that goes wherever I go. This is the short and simple truth of the good news that is True for everyone right now and forever.

If we ask, in complete honesty, what it is we are all looking for, I believe this is it. We all want to know the good news and where we can place our hope and faith without being disappointed. Much of my life I've spent feeling like I don't have enough, or am not enough, the way I am. I have wanted to have the feeling that *I have all I need.* Jesus said if we want something, we must believe, or feel as though we have already received it, for it to be made real. *24 Therefore I tell you, whatever you ask for in prayer, believe that you have received it, and it will be yours (Mark 11:24 NIV).* The way to have abundance in our lives is to trust in and feel the abundance. Meditating upon and feeling our lack creates more lack. Asking for abundance from a feeling of lack reinforces how we feel lacking and creates more of the same lack. Feeling the good news of God's goodness continually at work within us and in the world around us creates more of its reality.

A good synopsis of the good news is found in Romans 8:

28 And we know that in all things God works for the good of those who love him, who have been called according to his purpose. 29 For those God foreknew he also predestined to be conformed to the image of his Son, that he might be the firstborn among many brothers and sisters. 30 And those he predestined, he also called; those he called, he also justified; those he justified, he also glorified.

31 What, then, shall we say in response to these things? If God is for us, who can be against us? 32 He who did not spare his own Son, but gave him up for us all—how will he not also, along with him, graciously give us all things? 33 Who will bring any charge against those whom God has chosen? It is God who justifies. 34 Who then is the one who condemns? No one. Christ Jesus who died—more than that, who was raised to life—is at the right hand of God and is also interceding for us. 35 Who shall separate us from the love of Christ? Shall trouble or hardship or persecution or famine or nakedness or danger or sword? 36 As it is written:

"For your sake we face death all day long;
  we are considered as sheep to be slaughtered."

37 No, in all these things we are more than conquerors through him who loved us. 38 For I am convinced that neither death nor life, neither angels nor demons, neither the present nor the future, nor any powers, 39 neither height nor depth, nor anything else in all creation, will be able to separate us from the love of God that is in Christ Jesus our Lord. (Romans 8:28-39 NIV)

If it is true there is nothing in all of creation that can separate us from the love of God that is in Christ Jesus, then even the most vile and wicked of spirits or persons among us cannot cause any lasting separation. For the Spirit-Essence within all humankind is the True and lasting nature. Wickedness comes from not experientially knowing the True and lasting Essence within. Those whom God has chosen are all of us in our Spirit-Essence. For Christ is all and in all.

Our perspective and interpretations of the world around us are determined by our identity. If we experience ourselves to be our mind and body, all our interpretations and conclusions will be based on our mind-generated separate sense of self and others. On the other hand, if we experience ourselves as *no one* with any particular form or identity, we will see the world and everything in it from this Spiritual heart-centered oneness of Being. Because *Jesus Christ is the same yesterday, today, and forever (Hebrews 13:8)*, finding our identity in His constant, unchanging Presence in our heart-center is what will bring us the stability and confidence we have been seeking within the created and temporal world, but without success. For anything with only a temporary existence will only provide temporary comfort and stability.

Interpreting Scripture happens not only from our sense of identity, but also from an acquired knowledge and understanding of the language and symbolism. The stories within the Bible may speak of actual events, but at the same time, they also contain a hidden layer symbolizing the Absolute Truth of the Ever-Present Christ. Though Scripture may be useful in helping us to find the Truth of Christ, it can also create a dividing wall, such as it did with the Pharisees of Jesus' time. Christ came to destroy that dividing wall that blocks us from finding our True freedom in His very Essence and Being. *For he (Christ) himself is our peace, who has made the two groups one and has destroyed the barrier, the dividing wall of hostility (Ephesians 2:14 NIV)*. The two groups are those who are far away (Gentiles) and those who are near (Jews). His purpose is to create in Himself one new man out of the two, thus making peace. This is the same exact *one man* who is left behind when formerly there were two women grinding grain or two people lying in bed (Luke 17:34-35).

Through the crucifixion of the/our flesh, we all have access to the Father by One Spirit (Ephesians 2:15, 18). No longer do we need a mediator. God is One. For *a mediator implies more than one party, but God is One (Galatians 3:20 NIV)*. We have been made one through the divine body and blood of Christ, which is not of this created world, but the Holy Spirit that connects us all into one ever-present Spiritual body. The true dividing wall is our own human mind, split in half between the right and left brain, and presiding as the ruler and judge. But our hearts are undivided. Not only is our physical human heart undivided, but so is the Spiritual center of our being, which is eternal and not of this created world. Through the Holy Spirit, within our innermost being, the physical heart and brain are united, and the brain becomes open to divinely intuitive perception and understanding.

Here is the abbreviated good news message using a variety of passages throughout the Bible. All man-made interpretations must also agree and corroborate with these verses.

1. *Not only did Christ come in a flesh body two thousand years ago, His Light gives light to everyone coming into the world. (John 1:9)*

2. *"If anyone hears my [Jesus'] words but does not keep them, I do not judge that person. For I did not come to judge the world, but to save the world. (John 12:47 NIV)*

3. *For from Him and through Him and to Him are all things. [For all things originate with Him and come From Him; all things live through Him, and all things center in, and tend to consummate and to end in Him.] (Romans 11:36 AMPC)*

4. *For God has consigned (penned up) all men to disobedience, only that he may have mercy on them all [alike]. (Romans 11:32 AMPC)*

5. *He has saved us and called us to a holy life—not because*

of anything we have done but because of His own purpose and grace. This grace was given us in Christ Jesus before the beginning of time. (2 Timothy 1:9 NIV)

6.   *Now the Lord is the Spirit, and where the Spirit of the Lord is, there is freedom. (2 Corinthians 3:17 NIV)*

7.   *Christ is all and in all [everything and everywhere, to all men, without distinction of person]. (Colossians 3:11 AMPC)*

In light of this wondrous news, we might be tempted to shout it from a mountaintop, and to proclaim it for all the world to hear! And we are all free to do this if it is our way. There are other ways, as well, that we can proclaim this life-giving message. Words can sometimes divide us, and our intention is to bring greater harmony and unity into the world. My path of sharing Christ may not look like your path. There are many who have come before us, but our path and method of sharing Christ will be unique for us.

As we share, it is helpful to remember that *Jesus Christ is the same yesterday, today, and forever (Hebrews 13:8)*. Though He appeared in one specific body, and it is helpful to share about the person of Jesus Christ and what He did two thousand years ago, His Life is ever-present in Spirit yesterday, today, and forever. It is even more relevant to share about His grace and Truth at work and operating before we are aware and continuing into our awareness of His Spirit-nature within us. He is the same always. If He were not here in us when we were unaware, neither would He be present and alive within us when we are made aware. Take the time to contemplate all the wondrous things you are aware of now that you were unaware of in past days. We tend to see only the things we have interest in or habitually focus on from day to day. **So many seen things are overlooked. Imagine how much easier it can be to overlook what is always there, but unseen, within us.**

Because I now understand that other religions may also point to the same Essence living within all, and working within all of creation, I no longer feel traditionally Christian words are necessary to give others the good news. *For in Him, we live and move and have our being (Acts 17:28).* The "Him" is Christ, of course, but science or other religions may use other words to describe this Divine Biofield of energy holding us all together and providing the very stabilizing Essence of our existence. When Jesus Christ walked this earth two thousand years ago, the technologies and language did not exist to make a message like this understandable.

The bottom line is there is good news for everyone, and new language exists to make the message of Christ comprehensible, meeting people where they are at any level. Even the mentally challenged or very young can breathe in the breath of God without needing to go to seminary to learn how to interpret the words of the Bible. In fact, Jesus told us we must become like small children to enter the kingdom of heaven (Matthew 18:3). Do you think we've made it much more complicated than it needs to be, if this is the case? The thing is, as very small children, we don't have a personal flesh-identity. But as we age, we naturally take ourselves to be the flesh body and the voice in the head. Because of this errant identification that we all naturally develop, we all experience the troubles in this world (or the fire and wrath of God), which puts us through much stress until we consciously become aware of our inherent formless identity. Yes, it is true that we don't all discover this Spiritual identity within our lifetimes, but God has a bigger and better plan. He needs us all to play the roles we've come to earth to play. If we had no antagonists, or issues to challenge us, we would never wake up to the Truth.

The purifying lake of fire is continually at work within us. And in directly experiencing the Truth of Christ in our inner being and living from the kindness in our heart-center, we may not even need specific words to bring others to their aliveness in the center of their being. It's quite contagious. One awakened being, such as Jesus Christ, affects multitudes. Jesus Christ came two thousand years ago to set people free, and He still comes in our own flesh today to set people free.

If you, like me, have gotten caught up in attempting to do all the right things to earn brownie points with God or become more Christ-like, it's okay. You can keep on doing whatever you feel is best for you until you realize it isn't working for you. I've put so much pressure on myself to know and do only the will of God. But now I understand God's will is that we follow our hearts and learn from wherever it may take us, allowing others to do likewise. *13 [F]or it is God who works in you to will and to act in order to fulfill his good purpose (Philippians 2:13 NIV).* We can't somehow mess up the plans of God or go against His plans for us. He uses it *all*, not only for our good, but for the good of others. Yes, when we are unkind to others, it creates hardship for them, as well as ourselves, but God still uses this unkindness to help prove and show His nature within us. We can so easily miss it. I can remember being so upset about a great many things. Suddenly, without seeking it out, I have felt this great peace come over me. I didn't understand this was the peace of God and His Presence within me. Instead of staying with it, I went right back to my mind and fed the fire once again. It's okay, of course. God has used it all for good.

But now that we have been made aware of Christ's Presence within the center of our Being, we can continue to give more attention to this calm and stable beingness. We can stay here, as this beingness, for as long as we like. Though even if our attention shifts, there is a part of us that is still here to observe the shifting sand-like attention. We can do everything we normally do from this beingness. If we place more attention on the shifting sand-like ideas and concepts in our mind, and once again find our identity from our temporary-self apart from Christ, all it takes is a gentle reminder, and we are right back in our True and lasting identity, freed from the instability of the world. You may find yourself challenged to keep your True identity, but this proving of your True self is necessary so that you will seek and find peace with your whole heart, rather than your double-minded brain.

As Christ's Spirit cleanses us from identities that are impure and unlike Him, being temporal in nature, we will live increasingly from love, peace, and joy. From this vantage point, with wings like eagles, we will soar and not grow weary. We will be able to face life situations with new divinely inspired intuitive solutions. Remember, though, that none of this is accomplished in our own strength apart from Christ. Our righteousness is found in the stability of our faith in our heart-center.

Though we may not see kindness outwardly, fixing our attention on the constancy within (Christ) is what brings it into increasingly greater reality. Whatever we elevate, lift up, and give prominence to is what will become more real for us. For a time, what is temporal and generated in our minds will be given our worship and attention. But as these comforts fail us, one by one, Christ will be revealed in His glory, as the eternal and ever-present source of our Spiritual being. He is the same yesterday, today, and forever, and is the One who will set the world free, one person at a time, beginning with you and with me.

Endnotes

1. https://www.mvorganizing.org/what-is-the-difference-between-absolute-and-relative-truth/

2. https://digitalcommons.iwu.edu/cgi/viewcontent.cgi?article=1018&context=tis

3. https://www.mvorganizing.org/what-is-the-difference-between-absolute-and-relative-truth/

4. https://www.ncbi.nlm.nih.gov/pmc/articles/PMC5651927/

5. Braden, Gregg. *The Divine Matrix: Bridging Time, Space, Miracles, and Belief.* Carlsbad, CA: Hay House, 2008. p. 21.

6. Ibid.

7. https://www.energy.gov/science/doe-explainsthe-higgs-boson

8. https://pubmed.ncbi.nlm.nih.gov/31728781/

9. https://www.123helpme.com/essay/Compare-And-Contrast-Christ-Consciousness-And-Buddha-754253

10. https://journals.sagepub.com/doi/full/10.1177/0084672418825314

11. https://www.himalayanacademy.com/media/books/what-is-hinduism/web/intro.html

12. https://www.newworldencyclopedia.org/entry/Logos

13. Ibid.

14. https://www.heartmath.org/about-us/hmi-mission/

15. McCraty, Rollin. *Science of the Heart: Exploring the Role of the Heart in Human Performance. Vol 2.* HeartMath® Institute, 2015. Published at www.heartmath.org and https://pathwaystofamilywellness.org/Inspirational/the-social-heart-energy-fields-and-consciousness.html

16. https://www.dictionary.com/browse/name

About the Author

Having spent twenty-two years immersed in continual Bible study, extensive Bible memorization, and attending a wide variety of Christian and Messianic church services, Katy Jean Marzolf has uncovered a novel and simple perspective for interpreting biblical Scripture that is easily accessible by all and expressed in her first book, *The One Body of Christ*.

When not studying Scripture or writing letters of encouragement, Katy Jean can be found enjoying the majesty of God's creation through hiking, backpacking, and caring for her two young grandchildren. Katy Jean has three adult daughters and lives in Wilmington, North Carolina with her husband, Karl.

Continue the Conversation with Katy Jean

If you enjoyed reading *The One Body of Christ* and want to know more, visit:

www.TheOneBodyOfChrist.com

From the website you will be able to:

- Ask Katy Jean questions.
- Read current blog articles.
- Be the first to know about upcoming books and events.
- Book Katy Jean to speak at your next event.
- Subscribe to receive emails and special offers.